True Partnerships in SEND

Drawing from first-hand discussions and interviews, this essential guide offers an in-depth, realistic overview of bringing up a child with complex and specific needs to enhance current practice and collaborative work with parents.

This book supports the development of effective child-centred planning and family-centred approaches, by using the expert voices and lived experiences of parents to inform critical discussion and build the skills of professionals. Chapters provide strategies, guidance and suggestions to strengthen effective partnership work with parents, children and young people. Scenarios, key takeaways and questions for discussion are also woven throughout, offering a greater understanding of the barriers faced by parents of children with SEND and encouraging the reader to consider how they can more effectively co-produce with families.

True Partnerships in SEND uses the voice of the parent and their lived experiences as the basis for narrative, research and discussion and includes wider concepts that can inform positive parent-professional interactions globally. It will be essential reading for SENCOs, teachers and other education professionals working with children with SEND and their families.

Heather Green spent 20 years as a Primary Teacher and set up a specialist resourced provision for pupils with difficulties in accessing a mainstream curriculum. She was also SENCO, Assistant Headteacher and a Specialist Leader in Education (SLE) in SEND. Heather is now sharing her experiences of working in partnerships with families and professionals as a Senior Lecturer at the University of Chichester, UK.

Becky Edwards is a Senior Lecturer in Childhood Studies at the University of Chichester, UK. She is an award-winning children's Author and Co-founder of the Parent and Carers Support Organisation (PACSO). As a Primary School Teacher, Becky has taught autistic children, been an early years SENCO and used her understanding of partnership working to run a children's centre.

nasen is a professional membership association that supports all those who work with or care for children and young people with special and additional educational needs. Members include SENCOs, school leaders, governors/trustees, teachers, teaching assistants, support workers, other educationalists, students and families.

nasen supports its members through policy documents, peer-reviewed academic journals, its membership magazine *nasen Connect*, publications, professional development courses, regional networks and newsletters. Its website contains more current information such as responses to government consultations.

nasen's published documents are held in very high regard both in the UK and internationally.

For a full list of titles see: https://www.routledge.com/nasen-spotlight/book-series/FULNASEN

Other titles published in association with the National Association for Special Educational Needs (nasen):

True Partnerships in SEND: Working Together to Give Children, Families and Professionals a Voice
Heather Green and Becky Edwards
2023/pb: 978-0-367-54494-2

Teaching Reading to All Learners Including those with Complex Needs
Sarah Moseley
2023/pb: 978-1-032-11475-0

The SENCO Survival Guide: The Nuts and Bolts of Everything You Need to Know, 3ed
Sylvia Edwards
2023/pb: 978-1-032-21947-9

Cultural Inclusion for Young People with SEND: Practical Strategies for Meaningful Inclusion in Arts and Culture
Paul Morrow
2023/pb: 978-0-367-64123-8

Providing Relationships and Sex Education for Special Learners
Paul Bray
2021/pb: 978-1-138-48747-5

Inclusion: A Principled Guide for School Leaders
Nicola Crossley and Des Hewitt
2021/pb: 978-0-367-34528-0

Leading on Inclusion: The Role of the SENCO
Mhairi Beaton, Geraldene Codina and Julie Wharton
2021/pb: 978-0-367-42050-5

The Governance Handbook for SEND and Inclusion: Schools that Work for All Learners
Adam Boddison
2020/pb: 978-0-367-37003-9

The School Handbook for Dual and Multiple Exceptionality
Denise Yates and Adam Boddison
2020/pb: 978-0-367-36958-3

Creating Multi-sensory Environments: Practical Ideas for Teaching and Learning, Revised Edition
Christopher Davies
2020/pb: 978-0-415-57330-6

Dyslexia and Inclusion: Classroom Approaches for Assessment, Teaching and Learning
Gavin Reid
2019/pb: 978-1-138-48749-9

True Partnerships in SEND

Working Together to Give Children, Families and Professionals a Voice

Heather Green and Becky Edwards

Routledge
Taylor & Francis Group

LONDON AND NEW YORK

Cover image: © Maria Riese

First published 2023
by Routledge
4 Park Square, Milton Park, Abingdon, Oxon OX14 4RN

and by Routledge
605 Third Avenue, New York, NY 10158

Routledge is an imprint of the Taylor & Francis Group, an informa business

British Library Cataloguing-in-Publication Data
A catalogue record for this book is available from the British Library

ISBN: 978-0-367-54495-9 (hbk)
ISBN: 978-0-367-54494-2 (pbk)
ISBN: 978-1-003-08950-6 (ebk)

DOI: 10.4324/9781003089506

Typeset in Helvetica
by codeMantra

Contents

Acknowledgement

The authors of this book would like to express their deep gratitude to the parents who shared their stories and offered their raw and honest thoughts and feelings about their lived experiences. Thank you to Brian and Chris for their interesting chapters and valuable input.

Thank you to Ninesh, Adam and Jess, we could not have done this without you.

We hope this book provides inspiration and cause for reflection and evaluation as we run in true partnership in whatever direction we need to go…

Note:
Throughout this book, reference is made to "Parents" as a collective term for all those who care for, and are responsible for, children and young people. Parents, families and carers are the people who have the archive of an individual's life story.

The themes discussed within the book include key principles and concepts in SEND. These underpin and play an ongoing role in the dilemmas linked to structural changes in legislation.

List of Figures

List of Tables

Contributors

Brian Lamb is a consultant specialising in SEN and disability issues working with parents, local authorities and schools on the SEND reforms. Brian chaired the Lamb Inquiry into Parental Confidence in Special Education Needs (2008–2009). He is also visiting professor of Special Educational Needs and Disability at Derby University, an advisor to the National Sensory Impairment Partnership and a member of the Lead Group of the SEND Policy Forum. As the chair of the Special Education Consortium (2000–2010), he worked on all the key areas of legislation related to SEND. He has also served on a number of Government enquires including the Disability Rights Task Force (1995–1997), advisor to the Bercow Review into Speech and Language Therapy, the Ministerial Implementation Group on Aiming High for Disabled Children (2007–2010) and the Ministerial Working Group on Special Schools (2005). He has published extensively on SEN and disability issues and has been a School Governor in both special and mainstream schools. He worked for 25 years in the disability charity's Scope and the Royal National Institute for Deaf People in senior positions before becoming a consultant.

Chris Smethurst first left the education system with the intention of pursuing a career in aviation. This was not a success, although it may be some reassurance to nervous passengers that it is not Chris who is in charge of their plane. A "back up" dream of becoming a professional musician similarly came to nought. This led Chris to a dawning realisation that the voluntary, and occasionally paid, work with people was not a flash in the pan, particularly as he had been doing it since school. Like many people, Chris was drawn into health and social care work because of family experiences and had always been interested in the impacts of stress, fatigue and burnout. This was a thread he maintained through an otherwise convoluted career in community work, residential care for adults and children, youth work, working with people with learning disabilities, working in mental health services and in social work. In management roles and again, once he re-entered the higher education system, Chris developed training and support under the loose banner of "resilience". As a life-long contrarian, he is occasionally sceptical about the recent application of resilience in social policy, HR practices and the education system. Similarly, Chris also experiences imposter syndrome when talking about resilience to individuals and groups who have led far tougher lives than him. Consequently, the resilience chapter incorporates learning gained from working with diverse groups of people, including parents, refugees, people with experience of homelessness and addiction, older people, doctors, nurses, social workers, teachers, occupational therapists, volunteers, care workers, university students and primary school children.

Introduction

This book reflects current perspectives of parents of children with SEND. Based on discussions with, and case studies from, parents, it offers an in-depth, realistic overview of bringing up a child with complex and specific needs. It enhances current practice, exploring key themes, linked to SEND and supporting the development of effective child/person-centred planning and family-centred approaches. It uses the information from parents to support critical academic and professional discussion and to enhance the skills of professionals. It provides strategies, guidance and suggestions which strengthen effective partnership working with parents, children and young people. It is hoped that this book helps professionals and students to develop greater empathy and understanding in their current and future roles.

Parental narratives and experiences have been collected through case studies and discussions. These narratives are underpinned by theoretical concepts and academic perspectives ensuring clear links between theory, concepts, lived experience and practice. Key messages are highlighted, with suggestions as to how to develop more effective collaborative working and foster positive relationships.

It is only if professionals understand the journey parents travel that true partnerships can be formed. So there is no better place to begin this book than with the voice of a parent telling her story:

Bringing Up a Child with SEND: Considering the Whole Family

It's often said about parenting, that the days are long, but the years are short. I'm sure that's true for some.

It's 22 years now since Tom drew his first breath 17 weeks before his fragile lungs had expected to be put to work. He had a 5% chance of survival, and when over the next seven months in intensive care something could go wrong, it did. We said goodbye to Tom more than once.

Now fast forward from that room of tears, alarms and pain, from the ventilated 675g wisp desperately clinging to life and you'll find Tom, composed but rightfully pleased with himself and life in general. There's a newly earned Level 3 distinction under his belt and a secure place at university.

To those of you who know us, you may be forgiven for thinking: how the years have flown.
They haven't.

I want to say that it's been easy, that Tom was always supported and never let down by the system. That's what I want to say, and so does he, because when things have been good, they have been exceedingly so. But as we sit down and talk through all the wonderful people and places that helped give Tom the wings he needed to fly (sometimes flap a little) to where he is now, we are forced to remember those other things that weren't good at all. Those incidents, those brick walls and those institutions and systems and people that hurt, patronised, held back and damaged.

Yes. When we dare to look back, we can see the road stretching straight out behind us, unsurfaced and bleak in places. Sometimes there are wildflowers on either side, sometimes only dry veld, sharp stones and potholes waiting along the way.

It's just easier to forget the long fight to be able to breathe, eat, to finally leave hospital after almost a year, to roll over, sit up, stand, walk…

It's easier to forget that when the desperate battle to live was finally won, the real war began.

I don't want to think about that incredibly fragile four-year-old (who was actually only three) being forced to start school against all professionals' advice. Or to remember Tom's needle scarred little hands shaking each day as he pushed open yet another school door…and hoped

DOI: 10.4324/9781003089506-1

for a better day. Easier not to remember that three primary schools promised to deliver and then failed him hopelessly.

For me, there's an image I wish I could shake forever from my mind: That glimpse through the classroom window, of Tom (whose hands didn't work properly when it came to holding a pen) waving a picture printed from an ordinary colouring book at the ceiling, alone in the corner, while the rest of the class had a literacy lesson on the carpet.

This was his individualised support in motion.

I don't want to remember the all-consuming protracted stressful & expensive battle with the local authority to get a Statement of Special Educational Needs (forerunner to the Education and Health Care Plan -EHCP), the constant bullying at school, the never to be issued birthday invitations, the teacher who refused to use a simple picture calendar each day, that had been provided by another professional, because 'all the other children would want one and that's not fair'. (This incident was not an isolated one, I use it as an example of many simple changes that could have been made and weren't. Small tweaks that would have made it so much easier for Tom.) With pain, I remember all this, thinking that this is his life, the only childhood he'll have.

And I can't forget that brave little boy, long day after long week after long year, getting up every morning, steeling himself and going to school.

Fight, fight, fight. All consuming, exhausting, heart breaking expensive and damaging.

It's quite easy to hurt someone, to leave them broken, but incredibly difficult to restore the soul. Recovery is another matter entirely.

And it didn't have to be that way.

We know, because after those excruciating years, we defied the local authority and moved Tom to a specialist school. The fight continued literally to the week of Tribunal when the local authority agreed to fund him there. We happily provided the transport.

And this is when Tom's life really began.

He had about seven years there and emerged a healed, whole person, ready to enter mainstream college, where with determination and good support, he set about getting his English & Maths GCSEs. He embraced every opportunity offered to him, attended every ALL session, overlearning and extra tutorial and had a 100% attendance. He worked flat out, often late into the night and early hours, and now, five years later, he stands at this cusp, and we draw in a deep breath and hold it with him.

Has the road finally been resurfaced, we wonder, is the grass green on either side, can we stop checking for stones, animals in the road, reckless drivers?

An end and a new beginning?

We don't know but are hopeful. This time, it seems, support is coming to him. All through Tom's life, no matter how stony the road, how frightening the path ahead, he has held fast to any hand extended out to him. More than that, he has embraced support and fully engaged.

And in addition, there have been many heroes along the way. It's hard to unravel the years to find those nuggets that kept him going. Mostly, I know, that it's Tom who has held it all together, held firmly to the wheel through foul and stormy weather. As a family we've watched him with an exhausting level of vigilance, which I'm not convinced can be toned down quite yet. There's this delicate balance one cultivates between letting go and keeping hold; stepping in and stepping back; speaking up and keeping quiet. I suppose it's all about choosing one's battles.

And then there's those people, those many bright lights along the road, who did what they said they would and more, who cared and made the difference. You probably don't know who you are, but if you do read this, please know that your wisdom, your willingness to do the right thing even though time was short and resources scarce, sometimes just your simple kindness and compassion, was enough. You are part of this journey and instrumental in bringing Tom to this point where he stands poised for the next phase of his remarkable life.

Thank you. Thank you from the very bottom of our hearts.

Claudia Cavanagh

1 The Importance of Parental Engagement

Brian Lamb

Why Focus on Parental Engagement?

The importance of parents' engagement in the education of their children has been a constant theme in SEND policy since Baroness Warnock's seminal report concluded that "the successful education of children with special educational needs is dependent upon the full involvement of their parents: indeed, unless the parents are seen as equal partners in the educational process the purpose of our report will be frustrated" (Warnock, 1978, par 9.1). The report recommended that parents should be included in assessments "from the earliest stages" (Warnock, 1978, 4.29) and that "The relationship between parents and the school which their child is attending has a crucial bearing upon the child's educational progress" (Warnock, 1978, par 9.19).

There have been at least three distinct strands in the drive for greater parental engagement and co-production with parent and children and young people (CYP) with SEND in recent education legislation and practice:

1. **Parents as joint partners with professionals in working towards improved outcomes for children**. This has been part of a conscious move away from paternalistic models of parental involvement to parental engagement (Green & Edwards, 2021; Hellawell, 2017; Hodge & Runswick-Cole, 2018; Goodall, 2017).
2. **Service efficiency and effectiveness.** Focusing on personalisation and co-production will lead to more appropriate and effective provision of education and other services and will ensure better outcomes (Together for Disabled Children, 2011; DfE, 2015).
3. **Values and rights**. There is also a specifically moral or values dimension which can be summed up as "parents have a moral right, not a mandatory duty, to know and choose" (Fox, 2015, p.368). There has also been a more general movement to support parents and children's rights to a voice through rights-based legislation such as the Equality Act 2010 and the UN Convention on the Rights of the Child 1990 (Cullen et al., 2020).

These three drivers have all influenced the recent SEND legislation (DfE, 2014) but the aspirations for greater engagement have not always matched reality (Lamb, 2009).

The Impact of Parental Engagement

As Goodall (2018) has noted "It is not clear why the findings of more than 20 years of research about the value of parental engagement (for) … children's learning has for the most part been ignored in school processes and policies". The evidence for the impact of parental engagement on learning outcomes is significant and longstanding. Desforges and Abouchaar (2003) found that, "parental involvement in the form of 'at-home good parenting' has a significant positive effect on children's achievement and adjustment even after all other factors shaping attainment have been taken out of the equation" (Desforges & Abouchaar, 2003, p.4). While a review of the learning outcomes of vulnerable CYP found that ensuring "better learning opportunities at home and at school … reduced typical gaps in achievement between these students and those without such problems" (Voorhis et al., 2013, p.76).

Research has often found it difficult to identify and isolate which specific factors in the relationship between parents, the school and children contribute to enhancing attainment (Voorhis et al., 2013, p.79). While we know about the physics of parental involvement, we have lacked "the 'engineering' science that helps us put our knowledge into practice" (Desforges & Abouchaar, 2003, p.90). Conceptual confusion over different definitions of

DOI: 10.4324/9781003089506-2

parental involvement and engagement in the literature has also hampered the evaluation of specific approaches (Goodall & Montgomery, 2014; Harris & Robinson, 2016). Having noted these challenges there is an extensive evidence base on the impact of parental engagement on children's development, educational attainment and wider outcomes including systematic reviews and meta-analysis. These are helpful in identifying some of the key features of parental engagement which influence better attainment and wider outcomes which could be integrated into school's practice.

Evidence for Parental Impact on Attainment and Outcomes

Attainment and Parental Engagement

Parental engagement has been found to be one of the key factors in ensuring higher achievement and sustained school performance (Goodall, 2018). Harris and Goodall (2007) found that effective engagement to place where there was learning in the home, as opposed to general engagement activities. This is supported in a review which specifically examined the attitudes, aspirations and behaviours of young people and their parents in influencing educational attainment and participation it concluded that there is "a reasonable case that parental involvement is a causal influence on their child's school readiness and subsequent attainment" (Gorard et al., 2012, p.7). Of all the intervention strategies they studied enhancing parental involvement was found to be the only intervention with evidence of a full causal model leading to improved attainment (See & Gorard, 2013, pp.7–8). A meta-analysis of 51 studies found that "Parental involvement programs, as a whole, were associated with higher academic achievement" (Jeynes, 2012, p.706). While a recent review of 97 studies by the Education Endowment Fund found that "The average impact of the Parental engagement approaches is about an additional four months' progress over the course of a year. There are also higher impacts for pupils with low prior attainment" (EEF, 2021).

The Importance of High Expectations and Parental Support

A number of systematic reviews concluded that one of the key factors in securing higher attainment is where parental expectations or aspirations are high. Wilder (2014) synthesised the results of nine meta-analyses that examined parental impact and identified key strategies that worked across these studies. The results "indicated that the relationship between parental involvement and academic achievement was positive, regardless of a definition of parental involvement or measure of achievement" (Wilder, 2014, p.377). The relationship was strongest where there were high parental expectations for academic achievement of their children. This was found to be consistent across different grade levels and ethnic groups.

A systematic review (Boonk et al., 2018) also found that parental engagement in children's learning was associated with improved academic outcomes at all ages. The types of engagement which showed a correlation with academic achievement included high expectations or aspirations, communication between parents and school, parental encouragement for learning and reading at home. The strongest association was when parent engagement was focused on parents' expectations for their children's academic achievement (Axford et al., 2019, p.161). A number of studies have also found that enhanced learning opportunities, coupled with high expectations and continual parental support are positively associated with academic performance (Goodall & Ghent, 2014; Harris & Goodall, 2007). The focus on aspiration and achievement is especially important when we consider that for children with SEND it has often been the case that aspirations have been lowered in terms of what teachers and professionals have expected and communicated to parents (Ofsted, 2010, 2021; Blandford & Knowles, 2013).

> we all know what our children can do… encourage us to also dream

> (Robert)

How Schools and Settings Can Improve Parental Engagement

Higgins and Katsipataki (2015) reviewed 13 meta-analyses on how school-home partnerships can improve parental involvement and impact on school-aged children's cognitive and academic outcomes concluding that "PI [parental involvement], where school, family and community partnerships are developed to support and improve children's learning in school, offers a realistic and practical approach that has consistent evidence of beneficial impact on children and young people's attainment" (p287–288).

Assessing the approaches that schools and early years settings can take to improve children's learning through parental engagement a review by Axford et al. (2019, p.174) identified the following promising approaches:

- "supporting parents to help their children read via home and family literacy interventions;
- classroom and home-based summer reading interventions;
- good school-home communication, including via text message; and
- structured, targeted interventions for parents aimed at improving children's social, emotional and behavioural outcomes, which could support learning".

There is also evidence of programmes improving children's social, emotional and behavioural outcomes which may in turn lead to improved learning outcomes (Durlak et al., 2011). A review of approaches on behaviour in the early years (Beckett et al., 2012) concluded that there was robust evidence of the effectiveness of a specific behaviour and relationships intervention in improving child literacy. Another review concluded that "There is extensive evidence that parental involvement and engagement with children's learning linked to partnerships between the home and school, has immediate and long-term effects, regarding children's behaviour, social and emotional development, academic achievement and enjoyment of school" (O'Toole et al., 2019, p.71). Engagement with parents also secures benefits in terms of wider outcomes such as general motivation and recognition of non-academic achievements which increase confidence, improved engagement with school and stronger academic self-efficacy (Blandford & Knowles, 2013). Furthermore, research found that supporting parental engagement offered good value for money (Cummings et al., 2012).

The scope of these reviews is wider than children and families with SEND nevertheless, studies of children from disadvantaged backgrounds also suggest that enhanced parental engagement in their child's learning and good parent-school alignment improves achievement. It can be assumed, therefore, that this holds as true for children with SEND as it does for other groups of disadvantaged children (Gorard et al., 2012). It is important to recognise that the principles "for educating pupils with SEND are the same as for educating any other pupil" (Cullen et al., 2020, p.15).

The Importance of Parental Voice

The recognition of parent's central role and what they bring to the relationship with professionals and the school is crucial in securing the benefits of parental engagement. Parents bring their own expertise and knowledge around SEN and disability which can be invaluable to teachers in informing their approach (Schultz et al., 2016).

> I had prepared visual time tables, you know, I taught all of the staff about autism and so actually I knew all the staff individually and worked very closely with his key worker

> (Susan)

Engaging parents also allows for individual advocacy, therefore ensuring appropriate provision for SEND even where this is sometimes challenging (Hartas, 2008; Schultz et al., 2016). Schools which provide "bespoke forms of support" are more likely to engage parents in learning (Harris & Goodall, 2007). Transparency and joint working can also improve parental confidence and the working relationships between parents and schools, and parents and the Local Authority (Penfold et al., 2009; Boonk et al., 2018). This is supported by a rapid review of evidence on the best ways of supporting attainment for low-income families which found that engagement is most effective when "it is collaborative, builds strong relationships and focuses on learning; Schools meet parents on their own terms by tapping into their needs and interests, creating environments that feel comfortable to them and involving other members of their community" (Menzies, 2013, p.3).

It is the act of engagement which helps in ensuring greater levels of parental confidence, irrespective of the specific interventions. Research also suggests that parents often value the capacity of professionals to listen and respond flexibly over more formal aspects of the assessment and engagement process (Hodge & Runswick-Cole, 2018; Smith, 2022).

> I can see this from the teacher side, the children that I'm able to help the most are the ones where we can have a good open communication with parents

> (Hope)

For parents of children with autism, it was being listened to and taken seriously that was powerful in terms of gaining trust (Whitaker, 2007). Another study concluded that "it was not just what the school did but the spirit in which it was done that led to successful engagement" (Mutch & Collins, 2012, p.177).

> I think you come across a lot of people who are being a professional but they've almost been doing their job for too long, they've forgotten that for you this is very personal, this is very human and you're just another case

> (Tessa)

While research conducted as part of the Lamb Inquiry (2009) found that it was the act of engagement per se, not the specific intervention which may have followed, which gained parental trust (Peacey et al., 2011).

Barriers to Parental Engagement

Implementing good parental engagement also has to address the barriers that many parents of children with SEND face in working with schools and settings.

Schools and Settings

Strategies for encouraging engagement need to take into account parental capacity to work with the school. Parents who may appear to be disengaged may have "a high level of commitment to their child's education, which is not matched by the capacity to provide effective support or by the ability of schools to work effectively with parents" (Carter-Wall & Whitfield, 2012, p.4). Some parents do not realise that they have a role in their children's learning while others would like to get involved but do not know how to (Peters et al., 2007). Studies of parental engagement suggest that it is the school that is "hard to reach" not the parents and that parents need to know they matter (Harris & Goodall, 2007, 2008; Day, 2013; Crozier & Davies, 2007). An important predictor of parent involvement in the school is parents' perceptions of their child's school and the schools' approachability (Epstein, 2009, 2011; Epstein & Sheldon, 2016). Schools that made the most difference to improving outcomes are able to align learning goals and language used to engage parents better (Blandford & Knowles, 2013).

> We were included and we went along all the points, and they always asked for feedback beforehand which was good.

> (Dan)

There are many reasons why parents might be reluctant to engage with the school (Hornby & Lafaele, 2011) but there are also some specific considerations related to SEND. Parents who experienced learning or behavioural difficulties as children are likely to have less confidence in dealing with their children's schools and teachers. This can be exacerbated if the reasons for engagement are related to behaviour issues linked to the SEND need (Hornby & Lafaele, 2011). Variation in engagement will also depend on the nature and level of SEND need with parents whose children have higher levels of need, such as those with EHCPs, having higher levels of engagement with the school (Barlow & Humphrey, 2012). Some parents are unwilling to have their children labelled and therefore resist their child being designated as SEND even when SEN-Cos and teachers wanted to engage (Wearmouth & Butler, 2019). Conversely, parent's reactions to a dyslexia diagnosis showed how they used the designation to frame a positive narrative that gave them agency and more capacity to engage with professionals and secure positive outcomes (Ross, 2020).

Professional interaction with parents of children with SEND can also be a contested arena. Professionals who are accountable for the deployment of resources will often have a more powerful position in the process and in setting the parameters of what can be co-produced than the parents (Boddison & Soan, 2021).

> It felt very much that they were you know, overworked, probably underpaid, I don't know and … but also, would never write anything in their report that they knew that the local authority couldn't provide already
>
> (Nigel)

Co-production has also been associated with a risk of accepting poorer public services than otherwise might have been achievable (Bovaird, 2007). Where educational professionals want parents to be involved, they were nevertheless concerned about parents who gave too much input (Bezdek et al., 2010). Mann and Gilmore (2021) found that teachers were sometimes ambivalent or even hostile to greater parental engagement, citing unrealistic parental expectations on the time and support that they could commit. Teachers appeared to focus on managing the process related to the school rather than wanting more engagement. Teachers who want to support parental engagement also felt that many families are "hard to reach" or unwilling to engage with the school or setting. These factors were more pronounced at secondary level than primary.

A number of studies reviewing children with ADHD and autism have also been less positive about the impact of parental engagement. For example, a systematic review of parent–teacher relationships for children with ADHD (Gwernan-Jones et al., 2015) found that the relationship was conflictual with a feeling that "Mothers were silenced" with sub-themes resolving around parents having dashed expectations, parent–teacher conflict as the norm and escalating resistance on the part of parents to teachers' responses. While a review of studies of parents of children with autism found that parents and carers and schools can have quite different perceptions of the effectiveness of working together; while parents and carers believed they received little help or information, schools reported that they did communicate effectively (Roberts & Simpson, 2016). Professional resistance or concerns around parental engagement need addressing in any successful strategy. This suggests that a focus on parental engagement in schools has to be a whole-school approach with the support of the school leadership if it is to succeed (Goodall & Vorhaus, 2011; Blandford & Knowles, 2013; Hornby & Blackwell, 2018).

> The Head couldn't always come but the Deputy Head was always at reviews and she actually went on to become the Head. She was really good, really encouraging, just felt like a good experience.
>
> (Dana)

Gender and Engagement

Historically parental engagement has been predominantly mothers' engagement (Hornby and Lafaele, 2011). While there is evidence that gender roles are changing in parenting responsibilities and that mothers and fathers have similar levels of aspirations for their children's achievement, mothers' level of engagement remains higher than fathers (Kim & Hill, 2015). A systematic review of also concluded that encouraging fathers' positive involvement in their children's early learning was important in ensuring better outcomes (McWayne et al., 2013). Fathers of children with autism felt that they brought value as experts on their own children but had to "battle" to secure services and support from statutory agencies. (Burrell et al., 2017).

I don't even know how to help my son. You lie awake at night just thinking, you know what, would I call myself a good dad.

(Robert)

Fathers of children with multi-sensory impairment were found to be committed to engaging with formal mechanisms but were less engaged in informal ones (Pancsofar et al., 2021). There remain barriers for fathers' engagement (Hart, 2011) which means that strategies around parental engagement need to recognise the gendered nature of parental response and develop specific strategies to address this difference (Hart, 2011; Kim & Hill, 2015; Burrell et al., 2017). There may also be specific issues in relation to fathers' experiences and reaction in respect of being the parent of a child with SEND which need to be addressed as part of any strategy of parental engagement (Pancsofar et al., 2021; Burrell et al., 2017).

Social and Economic Issues

Middle-class families have a number of advantages in respect of dealing with other professional groups including being able to use the vocabulary of teachers, feeling able to treat teachers as equals and having access to resources which support parental engagement in schooling (Ross, 2020; Harris & Goodall, 2008).

it's just a classic example of you know inequality in societies being perpetuated.

(Nigel)

One of the challenges in developing effective parental engagement is to ensure that parental engagement is possible for wider groups of parents as the benefits of parental engagement are seen across groups not just among the middle classes (Harris & Goodall, 2008; Goodall, 2018). It is also important not to make assumptions simply based on socio-economic factors as reviews of parental attitudes have also found "that teachers and other professionals may underestimate the aspirations of socio-economically disadvantaged children and parents and not appreciate the importance with which school is viewed" (Cummings et al., 2012, p.4). This is especially important in the context of SEND where a disproportionate number of families are economically disadvantaged which can be directly related to the impact of the SEND needs on family income and opportunity (Shaw et al., 2015).

The Impact of Covid

The experience of the Covid lockdowns led to parents being more centrally engaged in the education of their children (Skipp et al., 2021). This has added a new dimension to ensuring that parents can feel supported in addressing the needs of their children when professional support is either not available or being delivered more remotely. While the experience of lockdown has been a negative one for many parents and CYP with SEND, it has also disrupted normal service patterns and ways of working, exposing flaws in the current system (Skipp et al., 2021; Ofsted, 2021; Ashworth et al., 2022). The disruption brought about by Covid may also point to new opportunities for engagement and development of skills that were not possible before through using online communication and different ways of working (Beaton et al., 2021). The experience has also established that "local learning partnerships, have been at work to find local solutions and positive outcomes for children and young people…" in which "improvisation, rather than a strict adherence to established processes and restrictive policies, is welcomed and valued" (Hellawell et al., 2022, p.164).

What Can Professionals Do to Improve Parental Engagement?

A fundamental part of parental engagement is being listened to and for parents needs and concerns to be understood. Parents also need to be supported to become engaged through the school being welcoming but then supporting parents in knowing how to be involved. Parental engagement must be active and deliberate, communally and personally based, culturally sensitive and developing over time. Goodall and Montgomery (2014) suggest that parental engagement can be characterised as the final point along a continuum from parental involvement to parental engagement, focussing on the triad of parent, child and school:

- Parental involvement with the school (agency of the school),
- Parental involvement with schooling (processes surrounding learning and the interchange between parents and schools' staff) and
- Parental engagement with children's learning (parental agency, choice and action).

The types of engagement may change over time, with parents of secondary school children taking on a "stage setting" role where they provide an important backdrop to learning and motivation (Harris & Robinson, 2016), rather than having the same direct influence on their children's learning and choices as when their children were younger. What is crucial in all these descriptions is recognition that good parental engagement is part of a planned process committed to by parents and professionals working together to support the child's learning.

There are a number of principles for effective engagement at the school level from the different studies which Goodall and Vorhaus (2011) summarised:

- Parental engagement strategies need to be part of a whole-school approach including active collaboration with parents
- Support activities must have the clear goal of improving children's learning
- There must be clear leadership within the school on parental engagement
- Sustainability depends on effective monitoring and evaluation of interventions.

Epstein (2009) identified a number of factors developed into a Framework of Six Types of Involvement. Epstein's typology can be applied individually but the optimal outcome is achieved through a combination of several types of involvement. Epstein identifies "overlapping spheres of influence", where schools, families and communities support each other. These are:

1. Parenting: helps parents to establish a stimulating home environment
2. Communicating: establishes effective interchange between school and family
3. Volunteering: parents as helpers and supporters at school
4. Learning at home: the school shares curriculum-related information and ideas with parents.
5. Making decisions: including parents in school decisions
6. Collaborating with community: identifies and integrates resources and services from the community. (Epstein, 2009, 2011)

The Structured Conversation

One approach to ensuring better parental engagement is the "structured conversation" (SC). It was piloted following a recommendation in an interim letter from the Lamb Inquiry (Lamb, 2008) as part of the Achievement for All initiative. The pilot combined a whole-school approach to improving progression and attainment for children with SEND with greater parental engagement and was the basis for elements of the approach in the school-focused chapter of the CoP (2015, sec 6.4). The parental engagement element of the approach was progressed through a series of SCs between the classroom teacher and parents which provide a platform from which parents could effectively engage in the learning process. The conversation allowed parents to discuss their aspirations and also share their knowledge of their child with teachers and professionals.

There were four key stages;

- **Explore stage** focused on a better understanding of the pupil and his/her needs, existing provision, what had worked well in the past and what barriers there were to achievement.
- **Focus stage** to be explicit about the nature of aspiration and need, to clarify key issues and their impact on progress, and to identify priorities.
- **Plan stage** parents and teachers to plan, agree and set challenging but achievable targets that addressed the key identified issues and may also be used for assessing progress. Parents would also be encouraged to contribute ideas for how they might support progress.
- **Final review stage** was used to summarise the key points of the meeting, clarify the next steps and arrange dates for further meetings or communication. (DCSF, 2009).

A review of the pilot concluded that parental engagement combined with a whole-school approach to quality teaching had raised pupil progression with all the pupils on the programme maintaining levels of progress above their non-SEN counterparts while attendance and behaviour also improved (Humphrey & Squires, 2011). Though it is complex to isolate the specific contribution of parental engagement within the overall approach, a follow-on study focusing specifically on parental engagement (Lendrum et al., 2015) found that the SC had led to:

- Constructive partnerships between parents/carers and the school community;
- Enhanced parent/carer, pupil and teacher aspirations for pupil achievement;
- Improved quality of information-flow between parents/carers and the school;
- Increased parental confidence and the ability to address barriers to pupil achievement and outcomes.

The approach was "effective in giving parents a voice that was listened to, changing the dynamic of teacher–parent relationships and allowing effective school–home partnerships to be developed" (Lendrum et al., 2015). It was noted that it was important to ensure that SCs happened at least twice a year but ideally more. In the research programme these conversations were usually once a term and for a duration of between half an hour and three quarters of an hour on average. It was found that "the frequency of SCs, the emphasis on giving parents a voice and listening to this, sharing the setting of targets and the focus on positive achievements" (Lendrum et al., 2015) were significant factors in improved confidence and progression.

Support for Professionals in Parental Engagement

There has been no national training or more specific support for teachers and SENCOs in implementing more effective parental engagement, although it is required by the SEND code of practice (DfE, 2015). Reviews of SENCo capacity have also raised significant questions about the time and support they have to meet the demands of the role which includes the engagement of parents as part of requirements of the CoP (Curran et al., 2019). An analysis of SENCO assignments for the NASENCO qualification found that working with parents did not feature as a major theme in the training (Esposito & Carroll, 2019). Another survey found that only 37% of mainstream schools provide training in how to engage parents and only 28% of school leaders had a plan of how to engage parents in schools. They also found that while 80% of schools recognised that parental engagement was the responsibility of all staff, the style of engagement and communication was too passive, with the assumption that staff already know how to engage parents effectively and that there is little follow-up of the outcomes of engagement activities (Axford et al., 2019). To address this, the authors proposed "providing staff with training and support in parent engagement (especially for so-called 'hard-to-reach' families)" (Axford et al., 2019, p.175). There also needs to be more explicit training for new teachers especially on overcoming cultural and economic barriers to engagement (O'Toole et al., 2019). This would build on a growing understanding of the importance of parents for school strategies (Hornby & Blackwell, 2018) and that "most teachers are genuine in their desire to actually find solutions and engage meaningfully with parents" often without the training needed to do so successfully (Hornby & Lafaele, 2011, p.46).

Summary

Good parental engagement provides one of the best opportunities for closing the achievement gap, especially in the early years for CYP with SEND (Fan & Williams, 2010; Voorhis et al., 2013; EEF, 2021). Good professional practice in schools and other settings should incorporate working with parents in focusing on children's learning not just engaging with the school or setting (Goodall, 2018). It is only by doing so that we can ensure that children with SEND are able to achieve better outcomes in line with legislative and parental aspirations. The case for parental engagement does not only rest on ensuring better attainment and outcomes, but also on the consequent increase in trust and securing of parental confidence. Parents and CYP have a right to be heard and included. Parental engagement requires a genuine exchange based on mutual recognition of what parents and professionals bring to help secure better outcomes, confidence and trust. It is only with commitment to the principles which underly good parental engagement that the benefits of this approach will be fully realised.

Top Tips

Goodall (2017) suggests the following principles for moving from the current ways in which parental engagement is conceptualised in schools to a more empowering model of genuine engagement where;

School staff and parents:

1. Actively participate in the learning of the child,
2. Value each other's knowledge,
3. Communicate effectively and meaningfully with each other and the child,
4. Work together as partners to support the child and each other and
5. Respect the rights and legitimate authority of each other's roles.

Discussion Topics

1. Does parental engagement risk turning parents into professional advocates and if so, would that be a problem and why?
2. Would it be worth investing in parental engagement if it did not show increases in pupil attainment and outcomes for CYP with SEND?
3. What is most important: gaining parental trust and engagement, or the delivery of interventions with the support of parents?
4. How could engaging parents of children with SEND be more effective, and how could this be measured?
5. What are the barriers within your own situation in implementing better parental engagement and how could you overcome these?

References

Ashworth, E., Kirkby, J., Bray, L., & Alghrani, A. (2022) *The Impact of the COVID-19 Pandemic on the Education, Health and Social Care Provision for Children with Special Educational Needs and Disabilities (SEND): The Ask, Listen, Act Study*.

Axford, N., Berry, V., Lloyd, J., et al. (2019) *How Can Schools Support Parents' Engagement in their Children's Learning? Evidence from Research and Practice*. London: Education Endowment Foundation.

Barlow, A., & Humphrey, N. (2012) A natural variation study of engagement and confidence among parents of learners with special educational needs and disabilities. *European Journal of Special Needs Education*, 27(4), 447–467. https://doi.org/10.1080/08856257.2012.711959

Beaton, M. C., Codina, G. N., & Wharton, J. C. (2021) Decommissioning normal: COVID-19 as a disruptor of school norms for young people with learning disabilities. *British Journal of Learning Disabilities*, 2021, 1–10. https://doi.org/10.1111/bld.12399

Beckett, C., Beecham, J., Doolan, M., et al. (2012) *Which Type of Parenting Programme Best Improves Child Behaviour and Reading? The Helping Children Achieve Trial*. London: DfE.

Bezdek, J., Summers, J. A., & Turnbull, A. (2010) Professionals' attitudes on partnering with families of children and youth with disabilities. *Education and Training in ASD and Developmental Disabilities*, 45, 356–365.

Blandford, S. & Knowles, C. (2013) *Achievement for All*. London: Bloomsbury.

Boddison, A., & Soan, S. (2021) The coproduction illusion: Considering the relative success rates and efficiency rates of securing an Education, Health and Care plan when requested by families or education professionals. *Journal of Research in Special Educational Needs*, 21(3). https://doi.org/10.1111/1471-3802.12545

Boonk, L., Gijselaers, H., Ritzen, H., & Brand-Gruwel, S. (2018) A review of the relationship between parental involvement indicators and academic achievement. *Educational Research Review*, 24, 10–30.

Bovaird, T. (2007) Beyond engagement and participation: User and community coproduction of public services. *Public Administration Review*, 67(5), 846–860. https://doi.org/10.1111/j.1540-6210.2007.00773.x

Burrell, A., Ives, J., & Unwin, G. (2017) The experiences of fathers who have offspring with autism spectrum disorder. *Journal of Autism and Developmental Disorders*, 47(4), 1135–1147. https://doi.org/10.1007/s10803-017-3035-2

Carter-Wall, C., & Whitfield, G. (2012) *The Role of Aspirations, Attitudes and Behaviour in Closing the Educational Attainment Gap*. York: Joseph Rowntree Foundation.

Crozier, G., & Davies, J. (2007) Hard to reach parents or hard to reach schools? A discussion of home–school relations, with particular reference to Bangladeshi and Pakistani parents. *British Educational Research Journal*, 33(3), 295–313.

Cullen, M. A., Lindsay, G., Hastings, R., Denne, L., Stanford, C., Beqiraq, L., Elahi, F., Gemegah, E., Hayden, N., Kander, I., Lykomitrou, F., & Zander, J. (2020) *Special Educational Needs in Mainstream Schools: Evidence Review*. London: Education Endowment Foundation.

Cummings, C., Laing, K., Law, J., McLaughlin, J., Papps, I., Todd, L., & Woolner, P. (2012) *Can Changing Aspirations and Attitudes Impact on Educational Attainment?* York: JRF.

Curran, H., Moloney, H., Heavey, A., & Boddison, A. (2019) *The Time is Now: Addressing Missed Opportunities for Special Educational Needs Support and Coordination in our Schools*. Bath: Bath Spa University.

Day, S. (2013) "Terms of engagement" not "hard to reach parents". *Educational Psychology in Practice*, 29(1), 36–53. https://doi.org/10.1080/02667363.2012.748649

Department for Children Schools and Families (DCSF), & The National Strategies. (2009) *Achievement for All. The Structured Conversation Handbook to Support Training*. https://dera.ioe.ac.uk/2418/1/afa_struct_conv_hbook_0105609bkt_en.pdf

Department for Education, & Department of Health. (2015) *The Special Educational Needs and Disability Code of Practice: 0 to 25 Years*. London: DfE and DoH.

Desforges, C., & Abouchaar, A. (2003) The impact of parental involvement, parental support and family education on pupil achievement and adjustment: A literature review. *DfES Research Report 433*.

Durlak, J. A., Weissberg, R. P., Dymnicki, A. B., Taylor, R. D., & Schellinger, K. B. (2011) The impact of enhancing student's social and emotional learning: A meta-analysis of school-based universal interventions. *Child Development*, 82(1), 405–432.

Education Endowment Fund. (2021) *Guidance on Parental Engagement*. Available at: https://educationendowmentfoundation.org.uk/education-evidence/teaching-learning-toolkit/parental-engagement (Accessed 27 May 2022).

Epstein, J. L. (2009) *School, Family, and Community Partnerships: Your Handbook for Action* (3rd ed.). Thousand Oaks, CA: Corwin Press.

Epstein, J. L. (2011) *School, Family, and Community Partnerships: Preparing Educators and Improving Schools* (2nd ed.). Boulder, CO: Westview Press.

Epstein, J. L., & Sheldon, S. B. (2016) Necessary but not sufficient: The role of policy for advancing programs of school, family, and community partnerships. *Journal of the Social Sciences*, 2(5), 202–219.

Esposito, R., & Carroll, C. (2019) Special educational needs coordinators' practice in England 40 years on from the Warnock report. *Frontiers in Education*, 4. https://doi.org/10.3389/feduc.2019.00075

Fan, W., & Williams, C. M. (2010) The effects of parental involvement on students' academic selfefficacy, engagement and intrinsic motivation. *Educational Psychology: An International Journal of Experimental Educational Psychology*, 30(1), 53–74.

Fox, M. (2015) 'What sort of person ought I to be?' – Repositioning EPs in light of the children and families bill. *Educational Psychology in Practice*, 31(4), 382–396.

Goodall, J., & Vorhaus, J. (2011) Best practice in parental engagement. *Research Report*. DfE.

Goodall, J., & Ghent, K. (2014) Parental belief and parental engagement in children's learning. *British Journal of Religious Education*, 36(3), 332–352.

Goodall, J., & Montgomery, C. (2014) Parental involvement to parental engagement: A continuum. *Educational Review*, 66(4), 399–410.

Goodall, J. (2017) Learning-centred parental engagement: Freire reimagined. *Educational Review*, 70(5), 603–621. https://doi.org/10.1080/00131911.2017.1358697

Goodall, J. (2018) Parental engagement in children's learning: Moving on from mass superstition. *Creative Education*, 9, 1611–1621. https://doi.org/10.4236/ce.2018.911116

Gorard, S., See, B. H., & Davies, P. (2012) *The Impact of Attitudes and Aspirations on Educational Attainment and Participation*. York: JRF.

Green, H., & Edwards, B. (2021) Working in partnership with parents. In M. C. Beaton, G. N. Codina, & J. C. Wharton (eds.) *Leading on Inclusion: The Role of the SENCO*. Abingdon: Routledge, pp. 141–151.

Gwernan-Jones, R., Moore, D. A., Garside, R., Richardson, M., Thompson-Coon, J., Rogers, M., Cooper, P., Stein, K., & Ford, T. (September, 2015) ADHD, parent perspectives and parent–teacher relationships: Grounds for conflict. *British Journal of Special Education*, 42(3).

Hart, R. (2011) Paternal involvement in the statutory assessment of special educational needs. *Educational Psychology in Practice*, 27(2), 155–174.

Hartas, D. (2008) Practices of parental participation: A case study. *Educational Psychology in Practice*, 24(2), 139–153.

Harris, A., & Goodall, J. (2007) *Engaging Parents in Raising Achievement: Do Parents Know They Matter?* London: DCFS Publications.

Harris, A., & Goodall, J. (2008) Do parents know they matter? Engaging all parents in learning. *Educational Research*, 50(3), 277–289. https://doi.org/10.1080/00131880802309424

Harris, A. L., & Robinson, K. (2016) A new framework for understanding parental involvement: Setting the stage for academic success. *Russell Sage Foundation Journal of the Social Sciences*, 2(5), 186–201.

Hellawell, B. (2017) A review of parent-professional partnerships and some new obligations and concerns arising from the introduction of the SEND Code of Practice 2015. *British Journal of Special Education*, 44(4), 410–430. https://doi.org/10.1111/1467-8578.12186

Hellawell, B., Smith, S., & Wharton, J. (2022) What was required above all else was collaboration': Keeping the momentum for SEND partnership working in the wake of Covid-19. *British Journal of Special Education*. https://doi.org/10.1111/1467-8578.12413

Higgins, S., & Katsipataki, M. (2015) Evidence from meta-analysis about parental involvement in education which supports their children's learning. *Journal of Children's Services*, 10(3), 280–290.

Hodge, N., & Runswick-Cole, K. (2018) 'You Say…I Hear …': Epistemic gaps in practitioner-parent/carer talk. In K. Runswick-Cole, T. Curran, & K. Liddiard (eds.) *The Palgrave Handbook of Disabled Children's Childhood Studies*. London: Springer, pp. 537–555.

Hornby, G., & Lafaele, R. (2011) Barriers to parental involvement in education: An explanatory model. *Educational Review*, 63(1), 37–52. https://doi.org/10.1080/00131911.2010.488049

Hornby, G., & Blackwell, I. (2018) Barriers to parental involvement in education: An update. *Educational Review*, 70(1), 109–119.

Humphrey, N., & Squires, G. (2011). Achievement for All national evaluation: Second interim report. Nottingham: DFE Publications.

Jeynes, W. (2012) A meta-analysis of the efficacy of different types of parental involvement programs for urban students. *Urban Education*, 47(4), 706–742. https://doi.org/10.1177/0042085912445643.

Kim, S. W., & Hill, N. E. (2015) Including fathers in the picture: A meta-analysis of parental involvement and students' academic achievement. *Journal of Educational Psychology*, 107(4), 919–934. https://doi.org/10.1037/edu0000023

Lamb, B. Letter to the Secretary of State December 8th 2008. Available at: http://webarchive.nationalarchives.gov.uk/20100202100434/dcsf.gov.uk/lambinquiry/

Lamb, B. (2009) *Lamb Inquiry, Special Educational Needs and Parental Confidence*. London: DCFS.

Lendrum, A., Barlow, A., & Humphrey, N. (2015) Developing positive school-home relationships through structured conversations with parents of learners with special educational needs and disabilities (SEND). *Journal of Research in Special Educational Needs*, 15(2), 87–96.

Mann, G., & Gilmore, L. (2021) Barriers to positive parent-teacher partnerships: The views of parents and teachers in an inclusive education context. *International Journal of Inclusive Education*. https://doi.org/10.1080/13603116.2021.1900426

McWayne, C., Downer, J. T., Campos, R., & Harris, R. D. (2013) Father involvement during early childhood and its association with children's early learning: A meta-analysis. *Early Education and Development*, 24(6), 898–922.

Menzies, L. (2013) *Educational Aspirations: How English Schools Can Work with Parents to Keep Them on Track Rapid Review of Parental Engagement and Narrowing the Gap in Attainment for Disadvantaged Children*. York: JRF.

Mutch, C., & Collins, S. (2012) Partners in learning: Schools' engagement with parents, families, and communities in New Zealand. *School Community Journal*, 22(1), 167–188.

Ofsted. (2010) *The Special Educational Needs and Disability Review: A Statement is Not Enough*. Manchester: Ofsted.

Ofsted. (2021) *SEND: Old Issues, New Issues, Next Steps*. London: Ofsted.

O'Toole, L., Kiely, J., McGillacuddy, D., O'Brien, Z. E., & O'Keeffe, C. (2019) *Parental Involvement, Engagement and Partnership in their Children's Education during the Primary School Years*. Dublin: NCCA/NPC.

Pancsofar, N., Petroff, J. G., & Schleppy, M. (2021) School involvement experiences of fathers of children with deafblindness. *British Journal of Visual Impairment*, 39(3), 239–250. https://doi.org/10.1177/0264619620921900

Peacey, N., Lindsay, G., & Brown, P. (2011) *Increasing Parents' Confidence in the Special Educational Needs System: Studies Commissioned to Inform the Lamb Inquiry*. London: Warwick University/Institute of Education.

Penfold, C., Cleghorn, N., Tennant, R., Palmer, I., & Read, J. (2009) *Parental Confidence in the Special Educational Needs Assessment, Statementing and Tribunal System: A Qualitative Study*. London: National Centre for Social Research for DCSF.

Roberts, J., & Simpson, K. (2016) A review of research into stakeholder perspectives on inclusion of students with autism in mainstream schools. *International Journal of Inclusive Education*, 20(10). https://doi.org/10.1080/13603116.2016.1145267

Ross, H. (2020) "It's a Battle!": Parenting and supporting a child with Dyslexia. http://dx.doi.org/10.5772/intechopen.93948

Schultz, T. R., Able, H., Sreckovic, M. A., & White, T. (2016) Parent-teacher collaboration: Teacher perceptions of what is needed to support students with ASD in the inclusive classroom. *Education and Training in Autism and Developmental Disabilities*, 51, 344–354.

See, B. H., & Gorard, S. (2013) *What Do Rigorous Evaluations Tell Us About the Most Promising Parental Involvement Interventions? A Critical Review of What Works for Disadvantaged Children in Different Age Groups*. Durham: Nuffield Foundation.

Shaw, B., Bernardes, E., Trethewey, A., & Menzies, L. (2015) *Special Educational Needs and Their Links to Poverty*. York: JRF.

Skipp, A., Hopwood, V., Webster, R., Dawson, & McLean, J. (2021) Special education during lockdown: Providers' and parents' experiences. *Research Summary*. NFER February 2021.

Smith, S. (2022) Overview of parental partnership: Assumptions, changes over time and consequences. *SENPRF Policy Forum paper*.

Together for Disabled Children. (2011) How Parent Participation and Parent Carer Forums leads to better outcomes for disabled children, young people and their families. https://webarchive.nationalarchives.gov.uk/ukgwa/20110302114211/http://www.togetherfdc.org/Topics/EvaluationImpactOutcomes.aspx

Voorhis, V., Maier, F. L., Epstein, M. F., Lloyd, J. L., & Chrishana, M. (2013) The impact of family involvement on the education of children ages 3 to 8. A Focus on Literacy and Math Achievement Outcomes and Social-Emotional Skills. October 2013.

Warnock, M. (1978) *Special Educational Needs. Report of the Committee of Enquiry into the Education of Handicapped Children and Young People*. London: HMSO; DES.

Wearmouth, J., & Butler, C. (2019) Special educational needs coordinators' perceptions of effective provision for including autistic children in primary and middle schools in England. *Education*, 3–13. https://doi.org/10.1080/03004279.2019.1664401

Wilder, S. (2014) Effects of parental involvement on academic achievement: A meta-synthesis. *Educational Review*, 66(3), 377–397.

Whitaker, P. (2007) Provision for youngsters with artistic spectrum disorders in mainstream schools: What parents say – and what parents want. *British Journal of Special Education*, 34(3), 170–178.

2 Models of Disability

The Great Debate

> I wouldn't change my child for the world but I would change the world for my child
>
> (Evelyn)

"Models" of disability can be understood as frameworks of ideas used to make sense of experiences in our social worlds (Cameron, 2014). A model is considered to be a particular way of ordering and structuring knowledge that helps us shape what is known (ibid.). Sewell and Smith (2021) suggest that, in the past, there was a dichotomy in the societal and professional understanding of difference and disability. The first, and initially dominant, conceptualisation has been defined as the medical model of disability (Oliver, 1990). This is an essentially scientific approach to understanding and classifying disability and difference, focusing on an individual's impairment, or diagnosis, as the reason and justification for their experiences in the social world. The second, the social model of disability, focuses on the social world as the source of the structural oppression and disadvantage faced by disabled people (Barnes, 2018). The social model has its origins in the civil rights and emancipatory movements of the 1960s. However, the potentially oppressive features of the medical model were first highlighted by Thomas Szasz's critique of American psychiatry, in the 1950s; it was Szasz who first coined the term "Medical Model" (Hogan, 2019). Whilst both medical and social models of disability originated in the last century, they continue to underpin the methods and approaches to inclusion today. An understanding of models of disability is useful if true partnerships are to be developed between professionals and parents.

This chapter explores definitions of the medical and social models of disability and other models of disability and considers how they are translated within policy and practice across the education, health and social care sectors. The way in which the models of disability are reflected in the practices of professional agencies will be presented through the accounts of parents. The impact on families will be considered alongside suggestions of how professionals can develop their effectiveness through enhanced knowledge and understanding.

The Medical Model

> the medical world was just looking at the disability, when everyone else was looking at the child and seeing her as an individual.
>
> (Tessa)

The above quote from a parent illustrates how the medical model places an emphasis on understanding disability through a scientific and medical lens. The medical model of disability takes a scientific approach to understanding difference, as a digression from a perceived "norm"; any behavioural variations from the "norm" can be categorised by a label, to become a condition or disorder (Sewell & Smith, 2021). The cause of such behavioural difference (disability) is seen as an individual problem within the person themselves. It views the cause of disability as being the result of something different within an individual's "biological functioning, with their physical body, cognitive processing or behaviours" (Sewell & Smith, 2021, p.7).

In the late 19th and early 20th centuries, the birth of Modernism created a way of understanding the world through a scientific lens. It is argued that Modernism determined scientific methods and approaches that were considered fundamental for human betterment and true knowledge about the world (Childs, 2016; Sewell & Smith, 2021). This scientific approach to understanding phenomena was also applied to disability. Scientific approaches to gathering information through observation and measurement were used, generating categories of disability. The medical

DOI: 10.4324/9781003089506-3

model view of disability as an *individual* problem perceives personal, functional limitations as impairments, whether they are congenital or acquired. When disability is understood in this way, resources are employed to provide a "cure" or to ameliorate the impairment. In this way, the individual is enabled to participate in the environment and society around them. This implies that to be disabled, is to have "something wrong with you" (Oliver, 1996; Cameron, 2014) which must be put right with appropriate professional support.

Cameron suggests that "What we know is learned and what we learn is moulded by the places and times where we find ourselves and by how these are explained to us" (2014, p.98). The most authoritative and frequently heard explanations should be those based on lived experiences. However, the loudest voices tend to be those which represent powerful groups of society, such as professionals and the media (Cameron, 2014).

One parent describes how professionals responded to the presentation of her newborn baby. Her experience illustrates the impact of how professionals can present their "scientific observations and measurements" (assessments) and voice their "explanations" (as discussed above).

> They wanted to put the thought [of diagnosed condition] in your head and I think all the joy left once that happened. I got the suspicion 20 minutes after he was born and any joy or any euphoria was just taken away. And then I had to think about it and you get your own perceptions of what you think the condition is and you have to kind of work your way through and navigate your way through [those thoughts].
>
> (Lianna)

It is argued that the expert knowledge of professionals, especially those in hospital-based, medical professions, is "disabling" (Barnes et al., 2002; Borsay, 2002). The parent cited above describes how they felt that, once the professionals involved had passed on their own judgements whether purposefully or sub-consciously, they had left her with the task of making her own sense of what the diagnosis meant.

The Personal Tragedy Model

The personal tragedy model is a cultural expression of the individual or medical model and is reinforced by messages that "able-bodiedness" is valued, whilst those "suffering" impairment are unfortunate (Cameron, 2014, p.117). The term "suffering" encourages a "pitiful" emotional response, suggesting the greater the "impairment" an individual suffers, the stronger the emotional response will be. Typical responses can be either pity or viewing the individual as an object of "inspiration"; a "hero", for being themselves (Young, 2014). Persistent reiteration of the perception that impairment signifies personal tragedy reinforces pressure on disabled people to disown any impairment and conform to societal expectations about normative behaviour, affect and attitude (Barnes, 2019). One parent describes the pressure of attending to the medical needs of disability and how that has the potential to become the primary focus.

> You sort of become obsessed by the whole medical world of your child and sometimes you forget that, yeah, they're just a child! Everything becomes that and [the professional] would go, 'oh, have you given her this to play with?' and I would go, 'no, I've been giving her her meds and her physio!...
>
> (Tessa)

The Social Model

In contrast to the medical model of disability, the social model perceives disability to be the consequence of environmental barriers and political and social issues. The aim of the social model is to undermine the idea that disability is caused by bodily impairment (Hodkinson, 2016, p.27).

In the 1970s, initial discussions that later formed the basis of the social model, began with the Union of the Physically Impaired Against Segregation (UPIAS) and The Disability Alliance.

"It is society which disables physically impaired people. Disability is something imposed on top of our impairments, by the way we are unnecessarily isolated and excluded from full participation in society."

(UPIAS, 1976, p.3)

This recasts the "problem" of disability as a social, structural issue rather than one of individual pathology (Cameron, 2014; Barnes, 2019). Consequently, it follows that impairments do not automatically lead to disability, but are instead exacerbated by how an environment is designed, or the manner in which a policy is exclusionary. For instance, a person may have a physical difference that leads to potential difficulties with moving in an environment, depending on how it is designed: a public building that has only stairs and no lift. This factor will exacerbate a physical impairment, causing the individual to be perceived as "disabled" (Sewell & Smith, 2021).

Initial constructs of the social model were extended in 1981 by the Disabled People's International to include people with sensory, emotional and cognitive impairments (Barnes, 1994). This provided a new framework for analysis and a narrative through which feelings of self-blame and personal inadequacy could be challenged (Cameron, 2014). It was clear that what was needed was the recognition and removal of physical and social barriers that excluded people from the mainstream. This required political action rather than "clinical treatment", "therapeutic intervention" or "nicer attitudes" (Cameron, 2014). Oliver (1990) argues that, since disability is culturally produced and socially constructed, individuals must be seen as people with equal, inclusive and inviolable rights as preconditions of a civilised society.

The social model provides disabled people with a robust foundation from which to advocate for equality (Cameron, 2014). It is a tool for making sense of the experience of impairment in a disabling society.

People are unbelievably uncompassionate. That's one thing that I have learned, is just how uncompassionate people can be. You just think, 'can't you just stop and let me push this guy in a wheelchair across the road?', they can't even slow down in their car....

(Matthew)

A criticism of the social model of disability is its lack of attention to the potential impact of any interlinked factors of inequality (intersectionality). However, there has been an increasing awareness of the significance of differences in experiences of oppression amongst disabled people, particularly on the basis of age, gender and "race" (Mercer & Hallahan, 2002; Barnes et al., 2002; Frederick & Shifrer, 2019; Raven, 2021). This challenges the notion of a homogeneous category of "privileged" knowers, which, in turn, focuses attention on contrasting and competing "knowledge claims" within the disabled population (Lawson & Beckett, 2021). Furthermore, the social model has been deemed to exaggerate the commonality of different impairment groups. It ignores personal experiences of impairment, such as physical pain (Swain & French, 2008).

you're putting together, you know a lot of apples, pears, bananas and fruit cakes, you know they are not the same and every child is so very, very different you can't lump them together but they are lumped together, so that's one of the hardest things. There's no such thing as special education needs, there's a bunch of children with you know, who are different from the normal for all different reasons, and you know, to lump them together under SEND is meaningless.....it is not treating the condition properly because they are lumping it into categories and pigeon-holing him inappropriately, so they're constantly banging him into a, ... you know, ... a round peg into a square hole.

(Matthew)

The Affirmative Model

Swain and French (2008) acknowledge, whilst tragedy has dominated views of impairment and disability, "authentic" writing by disabled people reflects a more varied and positive picture than disability as presented through less authentic, "able-bodied" narrative. The affirmative model is a way of thinking that challenges presumptions about the experiences, lifestyles and identities of people with impairments (Goldiner, 2022); it is a non-tragic view of disability which encompasses positive social identities and is grounded in the lifestyle and life experience benefits of being impaired (Sewell & Smith, 2021). Two parents describe how their children's disabilities can present "positive social identities" with a positive view of lifestyle and experience.

> Noel is not sexist, he's not racist, you know these are really admirable qualities.... I really admire the fact that he doesn't give a monkeys. I wish we could all share half that stuff.... to be able to start dancing in the middle of the cinema, and stuff like that.
>
> (Lianna)

> Like he is getting his tricycle not a bike and loads of people have said, 'well why doesn't he use stabilisers?' Well he feels the stabilisers are for kids, 'Oh don't take the trike to school because it will just make him look special needs,' Well he is special needs, but actually, he doesn't see it like that. He sees it as he's better off because he's got an extra wheel!
>
> (Hannah)

Cameron considers it is not the experience of impairment which is negative, but other people's response to impairment. The problematising of impairment by those identifying as "normal" involves a transactional exchange which validates their own sense of self (2014, p.6):

> They had been told by other students that you can take medication to get rid of autism, you just get a jab... Most children have the hardest time in secondary, but our children definitely [do] because that's when people start to build their opinions and they get their views of the world.
>
> (Evelyn)

The affirmation model makes the point that impairment is not an unfortunate, undesirable deviation from the norm, but a relatively common, ordinary part of human life. The model can be used as a tool for making sense of disabling encounters and interactions, such as described above. It can be a resource for disabled people to refuse to be what they are expected to become (Cameron, 2014):

> once I sat down and spent about an hour .... just explaining the ins and outs of it. And after he was like, 'oh I get it now.' And that's an example of somebody that actually listened and had a query, asked me, and I'm very happy to answer questions.
>
> (Hannah)

> You know what. I have stopped even explaining sometimes because it's just like, when things like that happen, I just pretend like I'm not there. The thing is we explain a lot to society, you know, we take care of society but they don't take care of us. So sometimes I just think I'm not going to explain.
>
> (Robert)

Robert's account suggests that the responsibility of "knowing" lies with society. The burden of responsibility to share information, and influence positive responses from society, should not have to lie with the parent or individual.

> when he was 1yr or 2yrs old, the hardest thing was, ... people's expectations and the fact that he has got to fight to be accepted from the start. But I don't think that's the case anymore, I do think things have changed... we walked past this chap on a motorbike, this kind lad and he walked by and said hello and nodded at Greg and said, 'alright mate?' Whereas I think back to when Greg was about 2yrs old and it was just people taking the mickey and being nasty. There are some people like that but not so much [now].
>
> (Dana & Dan)

How society interacts and responds to impairment and disability can affect an individual's psychological well-being. The affirmation model supports the labelling of an impairment as a difference to be expected and respected on its own terms, allowing a respectful stance towards disabled people's physicality.

Psychosocial Approach

The psychosocial approach considers an individual's psychological needs as well as the impact of their social environment (Wharton, 2021, p.154). Individuals are influenced by people around them: family, peer group, the wider society.

> you just feel that everyone is thinking that it would be so much easier if you just didn't bother and just go away and hide somewhere…

> ……the kids used to love Olive when she was little. [Our friend's] daughter is the same year group as Olive and their son is the same year as Timmy. And we knew them from Primary School in the city. When we got there (the Beach) we got Olive out of the chair so she could sit on the beach. There was a whole other group of teenagers and the Mum said, 'oh why doesn't Olive go sit with the other kids, why is she sitting with us?' So, we moved the chair and put it down with them and we were just chatting with the adults and Jono (Olive's father) said, 'oh god' and I said, 'what's the matter?', he said, 'well look over there.' And she was just sort of totally marginalised, nobody was paying her any attention whatsoever, and they were just totally ignoring her. Jono said, 'look let's… move her back up here (with us) or let's go and sit with her.' So actually, we went and sat with her. And it was just one of those moments where [I] just felt really angry … I just thought, 'fuck you. You've known Olive since she was a baby but now suddenly you're 16 and too cool hanging out in your bikini on the beach, so you don't want to talk to her.' It's just really upsetting actually and I just found myself feeling, you know, how excluded and judgmental people are. That was her greatest barrier, was other people's judgement of her, not her disabilities and I think that is true for many people. Why does our society make them think that's okay they can do that?
>
> (Tessa)

> I remember when Olive got her first powered wheelchair or had this special needs buggy, that did not look like any other buggy on the street, but particularly with the wheelchair, and people in the city would just stare at her and it was like, 'what the fuck are you staring at my daughter for! Stop it!' And little children would just be opened mouthed and just look, and they would make judgments about her because she obviously looks very disabled, and I thought, oh God yeah, …. you and your appearance, automatically [cause] a whole series of shutters or a whole series of categories [to] come flying down about what that person is like. I think I've got that sense very strongly with what it must be like to be judged on your appearance…… I wish people could really see Olive for who she is and what she's able to do and recognise the significance of that.
>
> (Jono)

Inclusion: Models in Practice

Inclusive Education

Inclusion means a number of different things to a number of different people (Hornby, 2015). The social model intends to liberate individuals from the social constructs of disability. However, within education, the universal interpretation of justice and equity and equality conflicts with this notion by interpreting "equity" and "equality" to mean "the same": the same school, the same class and/or being taught the same curriculum (Imray & Colley, 2017, p.16). Arguably, such conformist and reductionist interpretations of social policy and the principles of equality reflect the medical model. Educational settings are required to have "inclusive" provision in place as a precondition of "equality" in fulfilling their duty of meeting the individual's basic human right to an education; however, providing access to "the same' curriculum within "the same" education system does not necessarily meet the requirements of the social model in removing disabling barriers to educational attainment (Beckett, 2010; Cartagena &

Pike, 2020; Deacon et al., 2022). Parents interviewed for this book report experiences where their children, in the name of inclusivity, are in effect, "square pegs forced into round holes" (Matthew). Similarly, settings, which are specifically designed to be inclusive, may find this challenging if resources are insufficient to meet the child's needs (Hoskin, 2019; Paseka & Schwab, 2020):

> she was at a special language unit and suddenly not having any speech language therapy. We raised our concerns about that, but we were told that they had no obligation to provide it and of course at the time, her original special educational needs statement didn't specify exact amounts of speech language therapist, or time, or the nature of that therapy. So, it suddenly became clear that unless something was legal, you weren't going to get it. We ran into a problem whereby the teacher of the unit was concerned that her learning difficulties were too severe for her to remain in the unit and so essentially, they were going to kick her out of the unit. So, we realised then we were going to have to fight to keep her in the unit, and as part of that, we realised that the only way that you could get anything that was going to be guaranteed, was by making it a legal requirement for the local authority to provide.
>
> (Nigel)

This parent's experience suggests that the specific support needed for their child would need to be formally recognised and documented as a legal requirement for their child's individual needs to be met. In this way, they could exercise their rights and access a more equitable education. Yet, the social and economic policies of austerity have exacerbated a mismatch between aspiration, rhetoric and the realities of educational provision (Hoskin, 2019)

The Capabilities Approach

The "capabilities approach" recognises that people have different capacity, agency and opportunity to realise their human rights. In the case of a right to an inclusive education, as detailed in article 24 of the UNCRPD, it follows that an individual may require different levels of resources, support and advocacy (Reindal, 2016). The "capabilities approach" allows that disability and special educational needs (SEN) be viewed as an aspect of human diversity and difference, which necessitates a political response that prioritises entitlement to an inclusive education (Hellawell, 2019).

In order to access an education that has levels of resources appropriate for meeting the needs of a learner, within their individual's "capabilities", the current system requires a degree of scientific "measuring" (assessment) of the different resources required. This creates something of a paradox: in order to address disabling environments, the methods of the medical model are employed. Imray and Colley (2017) argue that assessments of need, employ a medical model which neutralises and negates the nuances of individual experience. The process of categorisation risks the individual no longer being viewed as a person, but as a "category" or "label" defined by their SEN (Imray & Colley, 2017). Nevertheless, the application of reductionist labels may be the prerequisite for access to services or support:

> We didn't have to fight for that, the health system just plugged us into the different things and we were invited to them. I mean we were just sort of being looked after.
>
> (Nigel)

However, the same parent describes their experience of meeting a barrier to accessing support within education because of the absence of categorisation or labelling.

> The other thing that is fascinating about special educational needs, is comparing it to health. If you go to your doctor with a lump, the doctor doesn't send you away and say, 'well if you can prove to me it's cancer, I'll pay for the very expensive treatment for you'. But in special educational needs, it's exactly like that.
>
> (Nigel)

Variations in Approach between Professionals

Both the medical and social models of disability form part of the planning processes for meeting the individual's needs. Within the constructs of education, health and social care, there can be significant variations in philosophy, policy and methodological approach. For example, one service may have a focus on prescriptive planning and another on responsive planning, meaning that a range of professionals use different assumptions and language which could impact on how and whether they work collaboratively. Such variations in approach have the potential to have an adverse effect on support for individuals (O'Connor, 2021) and be confusing and frustrating for parents:

> there is a whole load of different, 'ologies' you know, there is occupational therapy, physiotherapy, speech therapy, language speech therapy, eating therapy, play therapy, I don't know but this just goes on. I've got 15 of those, you know at any one time and they just do the same thing. They could just compile them together. The NHS has completely gone mad in all of these different 'ologies,' you don't need that many, you know, you end up being pushed from pillar to post with these people, which overlap massively in what they do and they all sit in different departments in different places, under different organisational structures, and accessing them all individually is an impossible task.
>
> (Matthew)

The levels of variance can also occur within the same professional group, but across different local authorities and health services (Gray et al., 2015; Crane et al., 2016). This can be problematic when people relocate to living in a different local authority from where initial assessment and planning of provision originally occurred. One parent describes the impact of this when they relocated from one local authority to another:

> we were living in the city, in a very poor borough and we had a really good team around [our daughter], what they would call an MDT, a multidisciplinary team. And we had an MDT far better than we've had [here]. Far, far better, and I think that's partly because there's more fluidity in the staff that goes through their systems in a big Metropolitan city....
> ....So there were quite a lot of Australian physio and OT's, who came with a different culture, different educational ethos around physio and more much more open and willing to listen to us. For example, there were things like splinting. We still kept all our care in the city and we would talk to the physios there and they would say, 'don't use splints. They are a waste of time. The evidence has just come out, you know over the last few years it doesn't make any difference.' And then the splinting was quite painful for [our daughter].....The physios [here, locally] they said, 'no, no, no, she's got to have them,' and we said, 'no, no, no she doesn't,' and we just in the end, ... it's really difficult you can't win, just have to kind of keep negotiating and negotiating and so there's a real problem there about evidence based practice, that sometimes you know you're really fighting against...
>
> (Jono)

Not only does this example from the parent describe the variance across local authorities, but also across cultures within a profession. There appears to be a stark discrepancy in service provision which appears to be dependent on where you live. (Legg & Tickle, 2019; Roman-Urrestarazu et al., 2021) In addition, certain locations naturally attract professionals from other cultures and backgrounds that bring a diversity of knowledge and expertise that can inform the possibilities of provision and support available.

Parents as Partners

Whilst the 'capabilities approach' recognises people are differently placed to access education, the process of working in partnership with professionals can cause parents to lack confidence in their capacity to act as equals. Tomlinson (2017, p.127) argues that parents as partners have often been inadequately involved and consulted, misinformed and overwhelmed by claims of professional expertise. Parents are expected to learn how to develop specific parenting skills by understanding psychological and neuropsychological concepts concerning the developing brain (Grane et al., 2022). Parents are lumped together as a homogeneous group, not accounting for any difference in their capability. One parent recalls receiving information with the assumption that, they were both able to access the information, and make sense of what they may find out for themselves.

> … we were given a label but we weren't given anything else with it. The only thing that they said to us was, 'just look on the NHS website'.
>
> (Jules)

Another parent describes the planning and preparation process they go through, in order to attend appointments and meetings with professionals involved.

> I think a lot of parents had the same experience of not understanding what was going on and so you would get these explanations but you still wouldn't understand what it meant or you would get a kind of explanation or some kind of medical terminology and often, if you were, for example, on [your] own with [our daughter] who was often distressed you know, through the reflux or whatever, [it is not always possible] to pay attention [to what the professional is saying], … whenever we had a meeting, we always went for two of us, so that one of us could look after [our daughter] and one of us could ask questions. Also, we would prepare questions in advance because we knew we weren't going to get the answers that we needed if we weren't well prepared.
>
> (Jono)

Research suggests that adequate information and supportive explanations of complex medical and policy concepts correlate with parents' enhanced positivity and resilience (Cadwgan & Goodwin, 2018; Reeder & Morris, 2021; Robinette et al., 2022).

The Role of the Professional

Whilst the social model of disability has led to changing views of the relationship between parents, families and professionals, these are often still shaped by the medical model perception that the professional is the expert. This can lead to the, often subconscious discounting of the unique and personal needs of those they are working with. Whilst this paradigm dominates interactions, with parents and individuals with SEND perceived as passive recipients of professional expertise, equal partnerships and trust remain elusive:

> there's always these little things where you suddenly realise that they are coming at it from their angle and you're coming at it from your angle.
>
> (Ava)

> I think you also come across a lot of people who are being a professional but they've almost been doing their job for too long, they've forgotten that for you this is very personal, this is very human and you're just another case…. I'm talking specifically about the medical world.
>
> (Tessa)

Community

Aligned with the social model of disability, diverse groups and organisations have formed to ensure that control of the future of disabled people rests with disabled people. Whilst the experiences and points raised in this chapter illustrate the fundamental role of professionals in partnership working, it is those with lived experience who are best placed to ensure future changes in legislation and policy provide equal opportunity for all, "Nothing about us without us" is a mantra that originated in South Africa's disability rights movement but has gained traction worldwide (Charlton, 1998; Franits, 2005). It is particularly relevant for the experience of disabled children and their parents discussed in this book.

As discussed at the beginning of this chapter, frameworks and models help people to make sense of experiences in our social worlds (Cameron, 2014). Communities can be considered a metaphorical "framework" where individuals come together, helping one another to make sense of their individual experiences within commonalities of the situation they may find themselves, e.g. parents forming support groups

> I think that you know for so many years, the support and the guidance that's available to parents, carers and the disabled, so much of it is hidden, or it is buried within these technocratic bureaucratic systems and kind of deliberately if I'm honest. Only those who've got that kind of tenacity and an educational level are able to access it. In this place, at [the school] you were able to share that expertise and share that knowledge, which was just really really important because often it was about, 'oh you can get this funding here, or a social worker here,' and so that was that was another aspect that was really useful.
>
> (Jono)

> ....I think the thing about the school was that it was a school for parents. I think that was a good name. So, it was about educating the child and the parent together and I think we had really good conversations with [other] parents about our children and that was so important and I think that's where there's a huge gap. Even though we have a massive online culture, I still think it's a problem of just having those kinds of small conversations around these issues.... where you can have that kind of, a bit more open discussion. I know that [there are] Facebook groups, we never were a part of that... So yeah I think school was a place where we found a lot of resilience and I think this is something that's really important, was that sharing of information and resources.
>
> (Jono)

It is clear from the experiences described here that informal communities created for parents and for those with disabilities are as important as formal collective coalitions and organisations. Much has been achieved in terms of information, resourcing and modelling through sharing their experiences, perhaps not always requiring the spoken word, but by just being present in the knowledge that those around you are also 'knowing'. This reflects the social model ethos where those with SEND gain agency based on vocalisation of shared experience and develops a sense of belonging

Ways Forward

To conclude this chapter, we look back at the models of disability and refer to the experiences of parents. We also consider their thoughts and ideas for changes that could be made for sustainable and equitable approaches towards disabled people.

The medical model situates the problem of impairment entirely within the individual. In contrast, the social model places the causes of disability in the environment and in political and social issues.

The affirmative model is a non-tragic view of disability, a way of thinking that challenges presumptions about the experiences, lifestyles and identities of people with impairments.

> Don't just see a patient, service user, student, see that person as a whole because we all know that children with Down syndrome have more in common with their family members than they do the rest of the whole Down syndrome community around the world.
>
> (Lianna)

The psychosocial approach considers an individual's psychological needs, how they are influenced by people and the environment around them.

> I wish that I could give people that kind of experiential understanding of what it's like. I suppose you can get that kind of ally-ship and stuff like that and various things do help with that, but I wish for a much more caring society.
>
> (Jono)

Despite the fact that the social model of disability has influenced the development of policy and legislation since its inception in the 1980s, the medical model continues to dominate much of the societal response to SEND. While various models of disability are recognised and acknowledged, the sense that impairment is a disability, rather than that disability is created by the response to impairment, remains a normalised societal view. Although current legislation is founded on the principles of the social model, approaches often reflect medical model values, both attitudinally and environmentally:

> let's make an accessible world; let's make buildings we can get into; buses we can get onto; entrances we can get through where even when you've got a level access there then put all the chairs everywhere so you can't actually get through; bus drivers who are going to stop being really grumpy because they have got to put their ramp down.
>
> (Tessa)

Five Key Take-Aways

- Models of disability can be understood as frameworks of ideas to make sense of experiences in our social worlds.
- The medical model places an emphasis on understanding disability through a scientific and medical lens.
- The social model places the causes of disability in the environment and in political and social issues.
- Consideration of intersectionality is important, avoiding the view of those with disabilities as a homogenous group.
- Informal communities are as important as formal collective coalitions and organisations.

Topics for Discussion

1. To what extent does legislation and policy reflect a medical model?
2. Which of the models outlined in this chapter best aligns with your experiences?
3. What would an 'ideal' model look like and do we need one?

References

Barnes, C. (1994) *Disabled People in Britain and Discrimination: A Case for Anti-Discrimination Legislation.* London: Hurst and Co. in association with BCODP.

Barnes, C., Oliver, M., & Barton, L. (2002) *Disability Studies Today.* Cambridge: Polity Press.

Barnes, C. (2018) Theories of disability and the origins of the oppression of disabled people in western society. In L. Barton (ed.) *Disability and Society.* London: Routledge, pp. 43–60.

Barnes, C. (2019) Understanding the social model of disability: past, present and future. In N. Watson, A. Roulstone, C. Thomas (eds.) *Routledge Handbook of Disability Studies.* London: Routledge, pp. 14–31.

Beckett, A. E. (2010) Challenging disabling attitudes and stereotypes. In F. Hallett (ed.) *Transforming the Role of the SENCO: Achieving the National Award for SEN Coordination*, pp. 126–132.

Beresford, P., & Wallcraft, J. (1997) Psychiatric system survivors and emancipatory research: Issues, overlaps and differences. In C. Barnes & G. Mercer (eds.) *Doing Disability Research.* Leeds: Disability Press, pp. 67–87.

Borsay, A. (2002) History, power and identity. In C. Barnes, M. Oliver, & L. Barton (eds.) *Disability Studies Today.* Cambridge: Polity Press, p. 132.

Cadwgan, J., & Goodwin, J. (2018) Helping parents with the diagnosis of disability. *Paediatrics and Child Health*, 28(8), 357–363.

Cameron, C. (2014) *Disability Studies: A Student's Guide.* London: Sage.

Cartagena, S., & Pike, L. (2020) Start with the end in mind: Frameworks for designing a socially inclusive school environment. *International Journal of Technology and Inclusive Education*, 9(2), 1559–1565.

Charlton, J. I. (1998) *Nothing About Us Without Us*. Berkeley, CA: University of California Press.

Childs, P. (2016) *Modernism*. London: Routledge.

Crane, L., Chester, J. W., Goddard, L., Henry, L. A., & Hill, E. (2016) Experiences of autism diagnosis: A survey of over 1000 parents in the United Kingdom. *Autism*, 20(2), 153–162.

Deacon, L., Macdonald, S. J., & Donaghue, J. (2022) "What's wrong with you, are you stupid?" Listening to the biographical narratives of adults with dyslexia in an age of 'inclusive'and 'anti-discriminatory'practice. *Disability & Society*, 37(3), 406–426.

Franits, L. E. (2005) Nothing about us without us: Searching for the narrative of disability. *AJOT: American Journal of Occupational Therapy*, 59(5), 577–580.

Frederick, A., & Shifrer, D. (2019) Race and disability: From analogy to intersectionality. *Sociology of Race and Ethnicity*, 5(2), 200–214.

Goldiner, A. (2022) Understanding "disability" as a cluster of disability models. The Journal of Philosophy of Disability. Available at: https://www.pdcnet.org/jpd/content/jpd_2022_0999_4_4_11

Grane, F. M., Lynn, F., Balfe, J., Molloy, E., & Marsh, L. (2022) Down syndrome: Parental experiences of a postnatal diagnosis. *Journal of Intellectual Disabilities*, https://doi.org/10.1177/17446295221106151.

Gray, L., Gibbs, J., Jolleff, N., Williams, J., McConachie, H., & Parr, J. R. (2015) Variable implementation of good practice recommendations for the assessment and management of UK children with neurodisability. *Child: Care, Health and Development*, 41(6), 938–946.

Hellawell, B. (2019) *Understanding and Challenging the SEND Code of Practice*. London: SAGE.

Hodkinson, A. (2016) *Key Issues in Special Educational Needs and Inclusion*. London: SAGE.

Hogan, A. J. (2019) Social and medical models of disability and mental health: Evolution and renewal. *CMAJ*, 191(1), E16–E18.

Hornby, G. (2015) Inclusive special education: Development of a new theory for the education of children with special educational needs and disabilities. *British Journal of Special Education*, 42(3), 234–256.

Hoskin, J. (2019) Aspiration, austerity and ableism: to what extent are the 2014 SEND reforms supporting young people with a life limiting impairment and their families to get the lives they want? *British Journal of Special Education*, 46(3), 265–291.

Imray, P., & Colley, A. (2017) *Inclusion Is Dead: Long Live Inclusion*. Oxon: Routledge.

Lawson, A., & Beckett, A. E. (2021) The social and human rights models of disability: Towards a complementarity thesis. *The International Journal of Human Rights*, 25(2), 348–379.

Legg, H., & Tickle, A. (2019) UK parents' experiences of their child receiving a diagnosis of autism spectrum disorder: A systematic review of the qualitative evidence. *Autism*, 23(8), 1897–1910.

Mercer, C., & Hallahan, D. (2002) Learning disabilities: historical perspectives. In R. Bradley, L. Danielson, D. P. Hallahan *Identification of Learning Disabilities: Research to Practice*. London: Routledge, pp. 1–65.

O'Connor, L. (2021) Social, emotional and mental health. In M. C. Beaton, G. N. Codina & J. C. Wharton (eds.) *Leading on Inclusion: The Role of the SENCO*. Abingdon: Routledge, pp. 65–72.

Oliver, M. (1990) *The Politics of Disablement*. Basingstoke: Palgrave Macmillan.

Oliver, M. (1996) *Understanding Disability: From Theory to Practice*. Basingstoke: Palgrave Macmillan.

Paseka, A., & Schwab, S. (2020) Parents' attitudes towards inclusive education and their perceptions of inclusive teaching practices and resources. *European Journal of Special Needs Education*, 35(2), 254–272.

Raven, S. (2021) Why does this matter? The value of intersectionality. *Cultural Studies of Science Education*, 16(4), 1137–1148.

Reeder, J., & Morris, J. (2021) Managing the uncertainty associated with being a parent of a child with a long-term disability. *Child: Care, Health and Development*, 47(6), 816–824.

Reindal, S. M. (2016) Discussing inclusive education: An inquiry into different interpretations and a search for ethical aspects of inclusion using the capabilities approach. *European Journal of Special Needs Education*, 31(1), 1–12.

Robinette, B., Palokas, M., Christian, R., & Hinton, E. (2022) Experiences of parents and prospective parents when receiving a diagnosis of Down syndrome for their child in the perinatal period: A qualitative systematic review protocol. *JBI Evidence Synthesis*, 20(12), 2995–3000.

Roman-Urrestarazu, A., van Kessel, R., Allison, C., Matthews, F. E., Brayne, C., & Baron-Cohen, S. (2021) Association of race/ethnicity and social disadvantage with autism prevalence in 7 million school children in England. *JAMA Pediatrics*, 175(6), e210054.

Sewell, A., & Smith, J. (2021) *Introduction to Special Educational Needs, Disability and Inclusion: A Student's Guide*. London: SAGE.

Swain, J., & French, S. (2008) *Disability on Equal Terms*. London: SAGE.

Tomlinson, S. (2017) *A Sociology of Special and Inclusive Education*. Oxon: Routledge.

Union of the Physically Impaired Against Segregation. (1976) *Fundamental Principles of Disability*. London: The Disability Alliance.

Wharton, J. (2021) SENCOs and social workers: working together. In Beaton, Codina, & Wharton (eds.) *Leading on Inclusion: The Role of the SENCO*. Oxon: Routledge.

Young, S. (2014) I'm not your inspiration, thank you very much: Ted Talk. Available at: https://youtu.be/ 8K9Gg164Bsw (Accessed 29 August 2022).

3 SEND Legislation, Parental Engagement and Co-production

Brian Lamb

Introduction

The Context

Education provision for children with SEND has reflected a culture of low expectations and a system that routinely fails to deliver the support that families say they need (Lamb, 2009, 2019; Ofsted, 2021b). Despite continual reforms to the SEND system children and young people with SEND continue to fall behind their peers at every stage of education, regardless of their prior attainment (DfE, 2022a). This has happened despite the ambition to support greater aspiration and achievement which has driven recent SEND legislation, policy and practice (DfE, 2011, 2015). The principles of involving parents have been integrated into successive iterations of the Warnock Framework with varying degrees of success and have culminated in the reforms introduced in the Children's and Families Act (CFA, 2014) which has created a strengthened legal framework for parental engagement (See Table 3.1).

Table 3.1 The Development of SEND Legislation and Parental Engagement

The Warnock Report 1978 stressed the importance of the relationship between parents and the school in determining children's progress, proposed that this relationship should be equal and that parents should be routinely consulted when children were being assessed.

Education Act 1981 introduced statements of special educational need and recommended that parents should be consulted on provision. Access to special education provision from 1944 to 1981 had been through the LA with no formal rights or channels for parents to disagree.

The Education Act 1993 and the subsequent SEN CoP (DfEE, 1994), later consolidated into the **Education Act 1996** included measures to ensure compliance with the requirements of the legislation on SEN and enhanced protections for children and young people. Parents were given the right to challenge LA decisions by establishing the SEN Tribunal, choice over the type of provision and the process of assessment was improved.

Excellence for all Children 1997 included a strong emphasis on the role of parents, good home school working and the importance of information for parents and promised further work on improving the SEN system. It committed to ensuring funding for parent partnership schemes which had to be established in all LAs.

Special Educational Needs and Disability Act 2001 strengthened the rights of parents to ask for mainstream provision while preserving the right to a special school placement. It established new duties for LAs to make arrangements for parent partnership services and dispute resolution between parents, schools and LAs through mediation. The Act also introduced new disability duties and required LAs to plan for greater access.

SEND Code of Practice DfES 2001 promoted a culture of cooperation as key for enabling children to reach their potential. Schools were required to recognise that parents have unique knowledge about their children and professionals (teachers, schools, Local Authorities and other agencies) and needed to work as partners with parents, and provide them with access to information, support and advice around SEND assessment and provision. It stressed that schools have a responsibility to fully involve parents in the various aspects of identification, assessment and provision.

Children and Families Act (CFA, 2014) and **Code of Practice 2015** replaced statements of special educational need with the EHCP. Created a legal duty to consult with parents at every stage of assessment and provision and in the provision and review of a EHCP. The Act creates the right for parents to be consulted on the strategic development of services in their area through the development of the Local Offer.

DOI: 10.4324/9781003089506-4

The Children and Families Act 2014 and Parental Engagement

Despite numerous changes to the statutory framework, it is only with the CFA 2014, that parental engagement was directly written into legislation as a statutory requirement. Enhancing parental rights was a response to continuing parental dissatisfaction with the SEND system despite the previous attempts at reform (Lamb, 2009, 2019). The 2014 reforms followed two Select Committee reports, a Ministerial Inquiry and Ofsted review which were all critical of the SEND system (HCESSC, 2006, 2007; Lamb, 2009; Ofsted, 2010).

The Act embodies the principles of parental engagement as the touchstone of its requirements in Section 19. LAs are required to have regard for "the views, wishes and feelings of the child and his or her parent, or the young person" and the importance of "participating as fully as possible in decisions relating to the exercise of the function concerned". This is then linked to providing the support to "help him or her achieve the best possible educational and other outcomes", (CFA, 2014, sec 19). The legislation represented a radical enhancement of parental rights to be consulted and listened to with the aim of delivering a culture change to whole system while staying within the overall Warnock Framework (Lamb, 2013, 2019). Educational need has remained the trigger for a statutory assessment and the reforms did not create any new statutory entitlements to health and social care provision. This has ensured that major fault lines between services have continued for many families (Norwich & Eaton, 2014; Lamb, 2011, 2019). Despite the emphasis on parental rights, there is also no model of co-production or parental engagement in the legislation or Code of Practice (CoP) (Boddison & Soan, 2021).

> with the LA ... it felt like an absolute conflict of interest that was always undeclared.
>
> (Nigel)

The Current Legislation

The current SEND legislation (CFA, 2014; DfE, 2015) creates two categories; "SEN support" or, if the child or young person has significant needs, a statutory assessment for an EHCP. Parents can dispute the refusal to assess for or provide an EHCP and also what is specified in the EHCP through the First Tier Tribunal which can make binding judgments on LAs about placement or provision. There is an important interface with the Equality Act 2010 which also confers significant rights to auxiliary aids and services, protection from discrimination and reasonable adjustments in the provision of services (Table 3.2).

Table 3.2 Summary of the Key Legislative Entitlements to Parental Consultation, Engagement, Information or Legal Redress (Updated from Lamb, 2018)

Level of Parental Engagement	Legislative and Statutory Requirements/Good Practice Requirements	Types of Engagement/Co-production
Schools and Service Settings	Consultation on the identification of CYP with SEND. Required to meet with parents once a year, should meet once a term as part of the graduated response.	SEND Governors, parent meetings, individual meetings with teachers and other professionals at school as part of SEN support process, contributing to the SEND Information Report.
	The Schools Information Report details what is provided by the school and its approach to SEND.	
	Ofsted schools level inspection/Ofsted/CQC area reviews on the implementation and delivery of SEND reforms which all include consultation with parents at different levels.	Feeding into Ofsted/CQC local area reviews.
	(Sections 29, 35, 66, 67, 68, 69, of the Children and Families Act 2014. Chapter 6 CoP 2015, Equality Act 2010, OFTSED Schools and Ofsted and CQC area reviews.)	

(Continued)

Level of Parental Engagement	Legislative and Statutory Requirements/Good Practice Requirements	Types of Engagement/Co-production
EHCP Assessment process and parental relationships with services and commissioning services	Duty to consult with parents/carers in assessment and the production of an EHCP and produce a personalised plan that takes account of their views.	Formal assessments for EHCP, ongoing meetings and reviews with parents, personal budgets, care assessments, other health assessments.
	Duty to discuss and potentially offer personal budgets. (Sections 36–50 of the Children and Families Act 2014; Chapter 9 CoP 2015.) Ofsted schools level inspection/Ofsted/CQC local area reviews on the implementation and delivery of SEND provision.	Feeding into Ofsted/CQC local area reviews.
Strategic LA-Local Offer, Health and Commissioning requirements	Duty to consult on the Local Offer. Duty to keep Local Offer under review and report on comments about the Offer by parents or CYP. Duty to consult on the joint commissioning of services.	Parent Carer Forums contribution to strategic and local planning, consultation with impairment-specific groups.
	Duty to consult on any proposed changes to SEND services.	Health and Wellbeing boards. Consultation on the Joint Strategic Needs Assessment. Parents groups and individuals.
	General duty to consult with parents in the delivery of services and produce better outcomes. (Sections 19, 23, 25, 28,29, 30, and 31 of the Children and Families Act 2014; The Care Act 2014; Health and Social Care Act 2012; Chapters 3 and 4 CoP 2015)	Individual comments from parents and carers on services and provision. Formal and informal feedback on the Local Offer. Specific service consultations and engagement on strategic working groups and boards.
Redress	Dispute resolution process. Right to have a mediation process.	Mediation and Dispute resolution. Individual assessment and adjustments, involvement and consultation in planning. Appeal to the Tribunal.
	Right to appeal to the First Tier Tribunal (FTT). Right to reasonable adjustments, auxiliary aids and other Equality Act protections (non-discrimination) which can be appealed at Tribunal. (Sections 51–57 The Children and Families Act 2014. Introduction to CoP and Chapter 11 CoP 2015), Equality Act 2010).	
	Local Government and Care Ombudsman can adjudicate on SEND legislation as this relates to the way authorities have carried out their duties under SEND legislation.	Appeal to the Ombudsman who can make rulings and order compensation.
Information Support and Advice	Local Authorities are required to support Parents and CYP with the information they need to make informed decisions. (CoP, 2015, Chapter 2). Local Offers to ensure that parents have the information they need about local services and support.	SENDIASS service in each LA is required to give impartial advice and support to parents.

Parents' Engagement at SEN Support

The graduated response is at the core of the approach to SEN support and follows a four-part cycle similar to the process in the structured conversation (DfE, 2015, par 6.4) outlined in Chapter 1. The code makes clear that "Consideration of whether special educational provision is required should start with the desired outcomes, including the expected progress and attainment and the views and wishes of the pupil and their parents". (DfE, 2015, par 6.40). It is then expected that the:

> "teacher and the SENCO agree in consultation with the parent and the pupil the adjustments, interventions and support to be put in place, as well as the expected impact on progress, development or behaviour, along with a clear date for review."
>
> (DfE, 2015, par 6.48)

The assessment should be reviewed on a regular basis as part of the graduated response with the opportunity to set clear outcomes and review progress. The school should meet with the parents three times a year (DfE, 2015, par 6.65). The "impact and quality of the support and interventions should be evaluated, along with the views of the pupil and their parents" (DfE, 2015, par 6.54). Further, it stresses that "they (schools) can also strengthen the impact of SEN support by increasing parental engagement in the approaches and teaching strategies that are being used" (DfE, 2015, par 6.66).

The guidance requires that discussions should be led by a teacher with good knowledge of the child, allow sufficient time to discuss all the issues and will normally be longer than usual parent teacher consultations. It notes that these conversations involve a considerable amount of skill and that staff should be trained in conducting the conversations as part of professional development (DfE, 2015, par 6.68). Where this approach has been followed, there have been significant benefits in respect of children's progression and wider outcomes as well as greater parental satisfaction (Blandford & Knowles, 2013; Lendrum et al., 2015).

> they were really welcoming and really clued up and we had regular reviews
>
> (Don)

Despite examples of good practice many schools have struggled with implementing the graduated response and clarifying for parents' what interventions and actions have been taken with children. Level of confidence in addressing SEND needs in schools is also low and leadership has been questioned (Webster & Blatchford, 2017). Surveys of teacher confidence have found that just over half (58%) of teachers found progress discussions with pupils' parents useful in developing the support they provided on SEN (DfE, 2020), while only 57% of teachers felt equipped to support pupils with SEND (DfE, 2022c). School closures due to Covid have exacerbated the issues around progression with three-quarters (74%) of school leaders feeling that the gap between children with SEND and non-SEND children had become wider, 31% reporting the gap had become much wider and 43% reporting it had become slightly wider (DfE, 2021). Parental lack of confidence in the offer for their children at SEND support has become a major issue in driving parents to seek an EHCP (NAO, 2019; Ofsted, 2021 a,b).

The Special Educational Needs co-ordinator (SENCo) plays a crucial role in liaising between the school, teacher and parents. Therefore, their responsiveness and commitment to parental engagement both for children at SEN support but also for CYP with EHCP's is crucial, though SENCos should not be a substitute for good teacher parent engagement (Green & Edwards, 2021). Early research suggests that SENCo's have embraced co-production and parental engagement despite the lack of specific training in this area noted earlier (Pearson et al., 2015). SENCo's routinely cite lack of time as a major impediment to being able to support families (Curran et al., 2019). The SENCo qualification is now under review which has brought uncertainty about the status and purpose of the role (DfE, 2022a).

Schools are also required to lay out their approach to SEND through their SEN Information Report which is a statutory document (DfE, 2015, 6.79). The SEN Information Report is the main accountability mechanism through which the SENCo and governors develop SEND policy and account for the deployment of the schools' "notional" SEN budget. Schools should ensure that the information is easily accessible by young people and parents and that it is set out in clear, straightforward language. The report is an exemplification of the schools' policy on SEND and could be used as a creative opportunity to develop and review the approach to SEND with parents. The CoP also makes clear that as part of the report schools should detail "arrangements for consulting parents of children with SEN and involving them in their child's education" and also "arrangements for handling complaints from parents of children with SEN about the provision made at the school" (DfE, 2015, par 6.79). Just under three-quarters of schools said they consulted with parents (73%) on the content of the SEN Information Report (DfE, 2020). However, it is not clear if the report is functioning well in terms of its' stated aims as many parents are still not aware of its existence (Ofsted, 2021a).

It came from top down, which is great in legislation but it needed to be from grassroots up.

(Leanne)

Education Health and Care Plans

One of the most significant changes of the 2014 reforms was replacing statements of SEN with EHCPs with the aim of securing a more personalised, outcome-focused and joined up assessment of need across education, health and social care with integrated commissioning across these services. EHCPs are triggered by an educational need with a requirement to consider health and social care provision. The Act requires that the views of children, young people and their families should be taken account of by health commissioners and other planning mechanisms (NHSE, 2017; DfE, 2015, 3.18–19).

Given the very heavy resource and professional expertise invested in EHCPs the engagement of parents is vital to ensure that needs are properly identified, aspirations captured and that parents and CYP can agree the EHCP with all the statutory agencies involved. This is especially important given the potential for different viewpoints about how needs are best met, including the best education placement, which may come with significant resource implications.

There are clear requirements for parental engagement in EHCP assessments throughout the process;

"Local authorities must consult the child and the child's parent or the young person throughout the process of assessment and production of an EHC plan"

(DfE, 2015, par 9.21)

The potential for conflict and different expectations is recognised with a requirement for active dialogue to be in place to resolve disagreements;

"At times, parents, teachers and others may have differing expectations of how a child's needs are best met. Sometimes these discussions can be challenging but it is in the child's best interests for a positive dialogue between parents, teachers and others to be maintained, to work through points of difference and establish what action is to be taken"

(DfE, 2015, par 1.7)

The enhanced levels of engagement have been popular with parents. In a large-scale study (Adams et al., 2017) of over 13,000 parents during the first stages of implementation of the reforms, 67% stated that their EHCP led to the child or young person getting the help and support they needed. Further, 66% of parents and young people expressed satisfaction with the overall process of getting an EHCP and 62% agreed that the support described in the EHCP will help to achieve the agreed outcomes. Three quarters (75%) of parents and young people reported that the process was family-centred. A follow-up study identified that close working with parents was a key positive factor and that its absence was a cause for concern in securing better outcomes (Adams et al., 2018). Another early evaluation found parents were generally positive about their experiences (Skipp & Hopwood, 2016) and recent reviews of implementation also noted the generally positive response to the engagement brought about by EHCPs (Sales & Vincent, 2018) but that there had been less success at including children and young people's views (Cochrane & Soni, 2020).

The changes to engagement in the process have not necessarily fed through into parents' perception of improved outcomes. A recent report by Ofsted which reviewed parental experiences in ten local areas found that the majority of parents in all the areas thought that since 2014 outcomes had not improved, they had not received the services necessary to deliver those outcomes and that education, health and social services had not worked together to deliver those services (Ofsted, 2021b). As each LA currently has latitude in how the plans are constructed and the process for assessment, there is inconsistent practice around the way in which parents are involved in plans and how well these are reviewed and implemented (NAO, 2019). It has also been questioned how far the current statutory assessment process represents co-production. Requests from education professionals were found to be 1.4 times more likely to result in an EHCP being issued than equivalent requests from families, suggesting that the system is still predominantly professionally driven. Further, the authors argued that the way co-production is currently framed creates expectations on schools' professionals that cannot be delivered undermining the pre-conditions of trust necessary for co-production to work (Boddison & Soan, 2021).

> I don't think we're at the centre, I don't think families are at the centre. I still I think there's still a lot of professionals making decisions people for people.
>
> (Tina)

There have also been concerns about the length of time to produce a plan, with only 59.9% of EHCPs completed within the 20-week statutory timescale in 2021 (DfE, 2022d), which has damaged the quality of engagement (Adams et al., 2017). While there is a clear legislative requirement to jointly prepare and commission EHCPs, this has not been routinely achieved or the legal requirements to do so enforced (Ofsted, 2017; HCESC, 2019). This has also damaged the potential positive impact that co-production could have made on the integration of health and social care with education and which could have also ensured a more effective use of resources (NAO, 2019). It has also been questioned how far this model delivers real choice for parents especially around the selection of schools. Satherley and Norwich (2021, p.12) found that most parents did not believe that they had "a 'real choice' of schools because there was a lack of options relevant to their child's needs" suggesting there are limits in the supply side with market models of choice for parents.

Personal Budgets

Personal budgets for education support were an innovation of the CFA (2014) and fit firmly within the consumer model of parental engagement. A personal budget can be requested by those in receipt of an EHCP and could be seen as the ultimate exemplification of one form of parental engagement and control. Personal budgets can offer a greater element of choice and builds on the co-production principles and trust in service provision, as they rely upon the LA officers and parents working together to agree on the outcomes for a plan and the funding to support that.

Critics have seen personal budgets as transferring more work and obligations onto parents, who have to manage a potentially complex set of relationships with multiple providers of services. There are also concerns that personal budgets entrench an individualistic and market led approach to the provision of services which does not allow for the aggregation of services across a number of children, especially where block contracts are used in the health services (Gough et al., 2014). There have also been concerns from parents that it has been difficult to disaggregate the provision through the personal budget from general provision for SEND within school settings and that "SEND provision was often shared with other students and was not ring-fenced" (HCESC, 2019, p.105). A study of SENCOs found that personal budgets are "seen as a withdrawal, rather than a redirection, of funds" (Pearson et al., 2015, p.15).

It has been difficult to integrate the educational component where access to specialist services is aggregated across a number of children. Only 2,186 out of a total of 25,259 personal budgets were directly related to payment of education provision in 2021 (DfE, 2022d). While the possibility of having control over commissioning services and managing their delivery is clearly valued by some parents there is little evidence, on current trends, that personal budgets will grow to become the predominant form of co-production and engagement within an EHCP context.

> don't put the emphasis on us to manage it, it needs to be managed for us, not us to do it… find an employee and pay their pension and set up a payroll. That is just all completely ridiculous.
>
> (Dana)

Strategic Engagement with LAs

The legislation requires that LAs consult with parents in the production of the Local Offer which is both a summary of what is available locally and a strategic planning tool to assess local needs and how best to meet these in consultation with parents and CYP. The Local Offer's role in engaging parents in strategic planning is central to understanding and changing the culture of provision by aligning needs and aspirations more directly with services and support (Lamb, 2013). Enhancing strategic engagement through co-producing the Local Offer has significantly increased the potential for parental influence in the strategic direction of the services provided by LAs (Lamb, 2013, 2018). The clear expectation is that:

> "effective parent participation can lead to a better fit between families' needs and the services provided, higher satisfaction with services, reduced costs (as long-term benefits emerge), better value for money and better relationships between those providing services and those using them."
>
> (DfE, 2015, par 4.13)

As well as co-producing the plan (DfE, 2015, par 4.9) there is a requirement to provide appropriate information of the services available within the local area. Limited formal accountability is also provided through a right to complain about gaps in services outlined in the Local Offer and make overall comments about the content of the Local Offer. The LA has to keep the Local Offer under review, respond to comments and publish them within a specified time period. The Government has been clear about the strategic role of the Local Offer:

> "we believe strongly that the Local Offer is far more than just a directory of local services and provision. We continue to encourage local authorities to use the Local Offer as a way of informing their decisions over future commissioning of provision."
>
> (HCSEC, 2019, par 76)

The potential of the local offer as a mechanism for co-production at the strategic level has been realised better in some LAs than others as evidenced in a number of reviews (Ofsted, 2021a, b; HCESC, 2019, par 216) and information provision has been poor in many areas (HCESC, 2019; NAO, 2019). Services did improve "where parents and carers had been given meaningful involvement in planning and decision-making.....In these, leaders had understood that co-production meant working with families as equal partners" (Ofsted, 2021b, p.18).

> I've experienced co-production… and I know what it feels like and how much stronger it's made me feel. It was about practitioners giving me a little bit of power, to have a bit more choice, control to help support my son.
>
> (Leanne)

The engagement with Parent Carer Forums has been mixed (Lamb, 2018), while there have also been questions about the adequacy of the information for parents and CYP in the Offer (HCESC, 2019). A consistent theme of the Ofsted local area inspections has been poor co-production in development of services (Ofsted, 2021b). Parents being co-opted to more formal planning structures also risks professionalising parental input and requires its own infrastructure of parent carer forums, professionalised behaviour and norms of working (Smith, 2022). Where this works well the forums can be a powerful influence for service improvement but there is a danger that they can also limit the range and scope of parental voices consulted to those who are most active and articulate locally.

SEND Information, Advice and Support Service (SENDIASS)

Every LA must provide or commission impartial, confidential and accessible information, advice and support services for children, young people and parents in relation to SEND. (DfE, COP, 2015, 2.17–19). This includes offering informal support to resolve disagreements and help in undertaking mediation, appeals to the First-tier Tribunal SEND and complaints relating to SEND. Issues of parent's access to information and understanding of the system have continued to be raised in a number of reviews (Ofsted, 2021b; Cochrane & Soni, 2020), which may reflect the continued complexity of the system rather than the efforts of local services to address parent's information needs.

> The system is absolutely stressing me to the limit of what I can understand
>
> (Dan)

Remedy

Disagreement Resolution Service

LA must commission an independent disagreement resolution service (DRS) for parents and young people. It covers all CYP with SEND. The DRS process pre-dates the current reforms and has been used as a means of deescalating conflict and reducing the number of Tribunals. However, research on a small sample of parents found that they had rarely heard of it and none had used it (Cullen et al., 2017).

Mediation Service

The CFA 2014 introduced rights to formal mediation if parents cannot agree with the LA about their decisions on statutory assessment with the aim of reducing conflict. Mediation and dispute resolution in this context can be seen as a formal part of parental engagement in that it still seeks to address parental concerns and find a solution at the individual level where agreement has not been possible. Before making an appeal to the First-tier Tribunal SEND, unless the application is about placement only, parents or young people must contact the mediation service to discuss whether mediation might be a suitable way of resolving the disagreement. Currently, the decision about whether to use mediation is up to the parents or young person (DfE, 2015, 11.13–11.38) but this may change given the reform proposals discussed below. A study of mediation found that it reduced the number of cases going to Tribunal and was cost-effective (Cullen et al., 2017). The use of Mediation has been rising, in 2021 there were 5,100 mediation cases held, an increase of nearly 1,000 cases from 2020. Of these, 1,300 (26%) were followed by appeals to the tribunal. (DfE, 2022b).

First-Tier Tribunal SEND

Where mediation has failed, or has not been taken up, parents can take a legal appeal to the First-Tier Tribunal whose decisions are binding on the LA. (DfE, 2015, par 11.45–49). These rights cover the Education element of the EHCP and limited legal coverage has been extended to health and social care provision after an extensive trial (IFF, 2021). Tribunal cases have grown from 3,147 in 2015 to 9,184 in 2021. While the total number of EHCPs has also increased this still represents a rise from 1.2% of all appealable decisions related to EHCPs immediately after the reforms in 2015 to 1.8% in 2021. This questions how far the system has become less adversarial (MoJ, 2022; Bryant et al., 2022). While legal redress is a crucial element in ensuring parental rights and voice within the process, it is more an indication that the other forms of engagement have not succeeded in addressing children's needs and parents' concerns.

> we felt.it was, us against them basically.... the only advocates for our daughter were going to be us.... and the only professionals we could trust would be ones that were not working for the local authority.
>
> (Nigel)

Local Government and Social Care Ombudsman

The Ombudsman can take complaints about the maladministration of services, including education services relating to SEND. Complaints cannot therefore be about the actual quality or type of provision but its remit can cover how decisions were arrived at, the timeliness of decisions and how well they have been implemented. The Ombudsman provides an alternative route for resolving certain types of disputes in SEND and can award financial compensation. The Ombudsman has taken a significant role in investigating EHCPs and has been critical of their operation (LGSCO, 2019).

Potential Future Legislation and Practice

The failure to successfully implement the 2014 reforms has led the DfE to review the system and bring forward a Green Paper "SEND Review: Right support Right place Right time" (DfE, 2022a) and an Education White Paper (DfE, 2022b) in an attempt to address concerns from parents. While it is difficult to anticipate which specific proposals will eventually be incorporated into legislation, they do give insight into the principles informing how the Government envisages parental engagement and co-production working in the future and the options and dilemmas the Government has in addressing these issues in the SEND system.

The Education White Paper proposed that any child falling behind in English and maths will have additional support, which is backed up by a parental pledge to ensure that "schools communicate this work to parents, ensuring parents are fully engaged in their child's education" (DfE, 2022b, p.37). This pledge also covers children with SEND who should "not need a diagnosis in order to access academic support" (DfE, 2022b, p.37). How the pledge is delivered within schools will be crucial and as there is no specific model of parental engagement being proposed it is difficult to evaluate what impact this commitment will have. A commitment to consult with parents on the learning of their child is significant in pointing towards a recognition of the role parents play in improving outcomes for children however implemented in legislation.

The SEND Review

The SEND Review Green Paper essentially accepts the criticisms of the implementation of the 2014 reforms. The solutions it proposes leave the architecture of the statutory framework mainly intact but introduces additional standards and accountability frameworks which include parents.

Co-production and Strategic Engagement

The SEND Review (DfE, 2022a) proposes a new national statutory accountability framework working with stakeholders including parents and carers with a number of specific mechanisms around strategic planning and accountability including;

- New statutory local SEND partnership boards including education, health and social care who will be required to work with parents to carry out an assessment of need and existing provision across their local area, identify the range of provision that will be needed to effectively meet those needs and produce an inclusion plan which will inform the Local Offer;
- Monitor progress on the inclusion plan through an Inclusion dashboard;
- Establishing new national standards across all areas of SEND provision including, "for co-production and communication with children, young people and their families so that they are engaged in the decision-making process around the support that they receive and the progress they are making" (DfE, 2022a, p.29);
- National oversight through a new SEND delivery board which will bring together relevant government departments with national delivery partners including parents and carers to hold partners to account for the implementation of the legislation.

The implementation of the changes is also dependant on "genuine and continual co-production with parents from local to national-level to ensure we implement the changes in line with our aspiration and as children, young people, and their families need" (DfE, 2022a, p.79).

In developing national standards for parental engagement, there are already models such as the four cornerstones approach by Rotherham (2020) which provides a framework for working with schools and settings and could inform the development of national standards.

The integration of parental engagement as part of the new accountability structure is important in meeting the statutory requirements on co-production and should help to ensure parents views are taken into account. How issues are framed and what is addressed or not addressed, as part of the process of co-production, is as crucial as simply having parents engaged in decision-making. There is a danger that co-production is undermined if parents are restricted to the parameters and funding decisions of a system which they cannot influence. The proposals also do not address a major fault line in the 2014 reforms as educational need remains the trigger for a statutory plan (Norwich & Eaton, 2014; Lamb, 2019). The legal underpinning for health and social care provision remains separate and the proposals try to address this through additional accountability measures (DfE, 2022a). Enhanced parental engagement on the new strategic forums is not necessarily going to bridge the gap in entitlements for provision in the underlying legal entitlements. There is also a danger that parents are co-opted into policing the SEND system through participation in accountability structures rather than creatively co-produce more appropriate services.

Individual Parental Engagement and Choice

The Green Paper is less supportive of parental rights and engagement if this leads to legal challenges to LA decisions and choice of provision. The main proposals at the individual level of engagement are:

- A requirement to undertake mediation before preceding to a Tribunal.
- Parents to be provided with a tailored list of settings based on the local inclusion plan, including mainstream, specialist and independent, which are appropriate to meet the child's or young person's needs when choosing a school.
- Creation of multi-agency panels to review EHCP decisions on requests for EHC needs assessments, the needs assessments themselves and the consequent placement and funding decisions that would have the involvement of parents on the panels.

These proposals are controversial as they are major restrictions on parental rights to redress and choice. Mediation is helpful in avoiding Tribunal cases and is cost-effective (Cullen et al., 2017). However, compulsory meditation reduces parental choice and risks increasing conflict. There is a potential imbalance between the LA and parents at mediation unless parents are well supported. Limiting choice around schools for parents is also likely to cause additional conflict if the local offer does not secure the appropriate provision. Pilot projects commissioned by the Lamb Inquiry (2009) trialled the use of parents on panels for statutory assessments, and they were considered a success in increasing transparency (Peacey et al., 2011). These proposals go further with panels reviewing the decision-making process and making legal determinations about provision, which may put parents in a compromised position of policing the system and adjudicating on provision (DfE, 2022a).

The Green Paper's proposal to hold schools to account for what is "ordinarily available" in SEND provision has potential in establishing a standard for parents of what they can expect in a particular school and to reduce dependence on statutory provision (Gray et al., 2022). Especially if the graduated response could be made more transparent about the support CYP receive and how they could be better engaged through individual planning and support before an EHCP. However, there is little focus on how parental engagement at "SEN support" is expected to be implemented or models of engagement.

Implications for Professionals

Whatever solutions the Government adopts teachers and professionals need training and support on parental engagement if schools are going to be more effective at including parents but this is not addressed in the Green Paper. Training on good parental engagement should start with initial teacher training (Mann & Gilmore, 2021; Pushor, 2015) and ensure that it is a part of continuing professional development (Goodall, 2014; Axford et al., 2019). Teachers and support staff also need time to properly engage parents and need to be supported by the school leadership (Axford et al., 2019). The approach developed by the structured conversation (see Chapter 1) could be integrated within the graduated response in schools as a way of enhancing parental engagement. Successful parental engagement is as much about being able to respond flexibly to parental needs and wishes based on the values embodied in the legislation as performatively following the regulations that are intended to exemplify those values (Lamb, 2013; Hellawell, 2017).

What Is Needed to Support Parents' Engagement in the Future?

Reviews of the Warnock framework since its inception all point to poor implementation as the major problem with improving provision without also considering that not enough attention has been paid to securing the change in culture, values and ethos that that is needed to underpin SEND legislation so that the system works for parents and children. As the Select Committee on Education concluded "Ultimately….unless we see a culture change, within schools and local authorities and the Government, any additional money will be wasted and make little difference to their lives" (HCESC, 2019, p.3). There are enough examples of where those values and commitment are in place to suggest that the changes can be made to work and that good parental engagement is key to changing the culture of provision and improving outcomes (Ofsted, 2021b; Lamb, 2019).

Legislation Top Tips

Legislation and standards can frame expectations of behavioural change but they are only going to be effective if the following are also in place;

1. Schools and settings secure a commitment to the values and ethos for parental engagement as well as the formal legislative requirements;
2. Schools and settings ensure that parental engagement is integrated into their SEND planning and reflected in their approach to the Schools Information Report;
3. Leadership is fully committed to work with parents in ensuring good parental engagement and makes sure that professionals have the time necessary to work with parents;
4. There are genuine opportunities for parents to engage at the individual and strategic level which meets parents on their own terms by tapping into their needs and interests;
5. There are agreed definitions and models of parental engagement which secure the support of both parents and professionals and are reflected in training and standards.

Key Questions for Discussion

1. Is following what is outlined in the SEND CoP is enough to ensure good parental engagement?
2. What one requirement in the SEND legislation is most important for your practice or situation and why?
3. How would you go about implementing the requirements of the SEND legislation on parental engagement in your own setting?
4. What are the major barriers to implementing the legislation on parental engagement from your perspective and what needs to happen to overcome these?
5. What is missing from SEND legislation to ensure that parents are fully engaged?

References

Adams, L., Tindle, A., Basran, S., Dobie, S., Thomson, D., Robinson, D., & Shepherd, C. (2017) Experiences of education, health and care plans: A survey of parents and young people. *Research Report*. London: DfE.

Adams, L., Tindle, A., Basran, S., Dobie, S., Thomson, D., Robinson, D., & Codina, G. (2018) *Education, Health and Care Plans: A Qualitative Investigation into Service User Experiences of the Planning Process.* Research Report. London: DfE.

Axford, N., Berry, V., Lloyd, J., Moore, D., Rogers, M., Hurst, A., Blockley, K., Durkin, H., & Minton, J. (2019) *How Can Schools Support Parents' Engagement in Their Children's Learning? Evidence from Research and Practice.* London: Education Endowment Foundation.

Blandford, S., & Knowles, C. (2013) *Achievement for All*. London: Bloomsbury.

Boddison, A., & Soan, S. (2021) The coproduction illusion: Considering the relative success rates and efficiency rates of securing an Education, Health and Care plan when requested by families or education professionals. *JORSEN*, 21(3). https://doi.org/10.1111/1471-3802.12545

Bryant, B., Parish, N., & Kulawik, K. (2022) Agreeing to disagree? Research into arrangements for avoiding disagreements and resolving disputes in the SEND system in England. *Isos Partnership*.

Children and Families Act (2014). London: The Stationery Office.

Cochrane, H., & Soni, A. (2020) Education, health and care plans: What do we know so far? *Support for Learning*, 35, 372–388. https://doi.org/10.1111/1467-9604.12316

Cullen, S., Thomas, R., Caton, S., Lindsay, G., Miller, A., Conlon, G., Caliandro, G., Peycheva, V. & Herr, D. (2017) *Special Educational Needs and Disabilities: Disagreement Resolution Arrangements in England Government report on the outcome of the review conducted by the Centre for Educational Development, Appraisal and Research (CEDAR).* DfE, MoJ 2017.

Curran, H., Moloney, H., Heavey, A., & Boddison, A. (2019) *The Time is Now: Addressing Missed Opportunities for Special Educational Needs Support and Coordination in our Schools.*

Department for Education. (1997) *Excellence for All Children Meeting Special Educational Needs.*

Department for Education. (2011) *Support and Aspiration: A New Approach to Special Educational Needs and Disability. A Consultation.* London: DfE.

Department for Education and Department of Health. (2015) *The Special Educational Needs and Disability Code of Practice: 0 to 25 Years.* London: DfE and DoH.

Department for Education. (May, 2020) *The School Snapshot Survey: Summer 2019 3. Support for Pupils Research Report.* IFF Research.

Department for Education. (2021) School and College Panel – October 2021 wave. *Research Report Authors.* IFF Research.

Department for Education. (2022a) *The SEND Review, Right Support, Right Place, Right Time..* London.

Department for Education. (2022b) *Opportunity for All: Strong Schools with Great Teachers for Your Child.* London.

Department for Education. (May, 2022c) School and College Panel – February 2022 wave. *Research Report.* London.

Department for Education. (2022d) *Education Health and Care Plans.* London.

DfEE. (1994) *The Code of Practice on the Identification and Assessment of Special Educational Needs.* London.

DfES. (2001) *Special Educational Needs Code of Practice.* London.

Education Act. (1981). London: HMSO.

Education Act. (1993). London: HMSO.

Education Act. (1996). London: HMSO.

Equality Act. (2010). London: HMSO.

Goodall, J., & Montgomery, C. (2014) Parental involvement to parental engagement: a continuum. *Educational Review*, 66(4), 399–410.

Gough, S., Dryden, S., Wolff, T., & Williams, J. (2014) Did we aim high enough? Will legislation lead to better results for disabled children? *Paediatrics and Child Health*, 24(8), 355–361.

Gray, P., Richardson, P., & Tanton, P. (2022) High needs budgets: Effective management in local authorities. *Government Social Research.*

Green, H., & Edwards, B. (2021) Working in partnership with parents. In: M. C. Beaton, G. N. Codina, & J. C. Wharton (eds.) *Leading on Inclusion: The Role of the SENCO.* Abingdon: Routledge, pp. 141–151.

Hellawell, B. (2017) A review of parent-professional partnerships and some new obligations and concerns arising from the introduction of the SEND Code of Practice 2015. *British Journal of Special Education*, 44(4), 410–430. https://doi.org/10.1111/1467-8578.12186

House of Commons Education and Skills Select Committee (HCESSC). (2006) *Special Educational Needs Third Report of Session 2005–06*. Volume I. House of Commons.

House of Commons Education and Skills Select Committee (HCESSC). (2007) *Special Educational Needs: Assessment and Funding: Tenth Report of Session 2006–07*. House of Commons.

House of Commons Education Select Committee (HCESC). (2019) *Special Educational Needs and Disabilities. First Report of Session 2019*. House of Commons.

Lamb, B. (2009) *Lamb Inquiry, Special Educational Needs and Parental Confidence*. DCFS.

Lamb, B. (2011) Support and aspiration: Cultural revolution or pragmatic evolution? *Journal of Research in Special Educational Needs*, 12, 107–121.

Lamb, B. (2013) Accountability the local offer and SEND reform: A cultural revolution? *Journal of Research in Special Educational Needs*, 15(1), 70–75.

Lamb, B. (2018) The SEND reforms and parental confidence: Are the reforms achieving greater parental confidence in the SEND system? In SEN Policy Research Forum. An early review of the new SEN/ disability policy and legislation. *Journal of Research in Special Educational Needs*, 18(3), 160–169.

Lamb, B. (2019) Statutory assessment for special educational needs and the Warnock report: The first 40 years. *Frontiers in Education*. Available at: www.frontiersin.org/articles/10.3389/feduc.2019.00051/full

Lendrum, A., Barlow, A., & Humphrey, N. (2015) Developing positive school-home relationships through structured conversations with parents of learners with special educational needs and disabilities (SEND). *Journal of Research in Special Educational Needs*, 15(2), 87–96.

Local Government and Social Care Ombudsman. (2019) *Not Going to Plan? Education Health and Care Plans Two Years On*. Coventry: Local Government and Social Care Ombudsman.

Mann, G., & Gilmore, L. (2021) Barriers to positive parent-teacher partnerships: The views of parents and teachers in an inclusive education context. *International Journal of Inclusive Education*. https://doi.org/10.1080/13603116.2021.1900426

Ministry of Justice. (2022) *Tribunal Statistics Quarterly: January to March 2022, SEND Tribunal Tables*.

National Audit Office. (2019) *Support for Pupils with Special Educational Needs and Disabilities in England*. London: NAO.

National Health Service England/Department for Education. (2016) *Guidance for Health Services for Children and Young People with Special Educational Needs and Disability (SEND)*. National Health Service England/Department for Education.

Norwich, B., & Eaton, A. (2014) The new special educational needs (SEN) legislation in England and implications for services for children and young people with social, emotional and behavioural difficulties. *Emotional and Behavioural Difficulties*, 20, 117–132. https://doi.org/10.1080/13632752.2014.989056

Ofsted. (2010) *The Special Educational Needs and Disability Review: A Statement Is Not Enough*. Manchester: Ofsted.

Ofsted and Care Quality Commission. (2017) *Local Area SEND Inspections: One Year On*. Manchester: Ofsted.

Ofsted. (2021a) *Supporting SEND*.

Ofsted. (2021b) *SEND: Old Issues, New Issues, Next Steps*.

Peacey, N., Lindsay, G., & Brown, P. (2011) *Increasing Parents' Confidence in the Special Educational Needs System: Studies Commissioned to Inform the Lamb Inquiry*. Warwick University/Institute of Education.

Pearson, S., Mitchell, R., & Rapti, M. (2015) 'I will be "fighting" even more for pupils with SEN': SEN-COs' role predictions in the changing English policy context. *Journal of Research in Special Educational Needs*, 15(1), 48–56.

Pushor, D. (2015) Walking alongside: A pedagogy of working with parents and family in Canada. In Orland-Barak, L., & Craig, C. (eds.) *International Teacher Education: Promising Pedagogies (Part B)*. Bingley: Emerald Group Publishing Limited, pp. 233–251.

Rotherham Charter. (2022) Available at: https://www.rpcf.co.uk/rotherham-charter-genuine-partnerships

Sales, N., & Vincent, K. (2018) Strengths and limitations of the Education, Health and Care plan process from a range of professional and family perspectives. *British Journal of Special Education*, 45(1), 61–80.

Satherley, D., & Norwich, B. (2021) Parents' experiences of choosing a special school for their children. *European Journal of Special Needs Education*, https://doi.org/10.1080/08856257.2021.1967298

Skipp, A., & Hopwood, V. (2016) *Mapping User Experiences of the Education, Health and Care Process: A Qualitative Study*. London: DfE.

Smith, S. (2022) Overview of parental partnership: assumptions, changes over time and consequences. *SENPRF Policy Forum Paper*.

Warnock, M. (1978) *Special Educational Needs. Report of the Committee of Enquiry into the Education of Handicapped Children and Young People*. London: HMSO; DES.

Webster, R., & Blatchford, P. (2017) *The Special Educational Needs in Secondary Education (SENSE) Study: Final Report – A Study of the Teaching and Support Experienced by Pupils with Statements and Education, Health and Care Plans in Mainstream and Special Schools*. London: Nuffield Foundation.

4   Relevant Theories and Concepts

Introduction

The study of disability, its impact on those with impairments and their families and the way in which society interacts with them has been a developing field of academic interest since the 1960s. With the emergence of the Union of the Physically Impaired Against Segregation (UPIAS) in the 1970s and, subsequently, of critically respected and influential academics, who write and talk about their personal experiences of disability, concepts and theories have come to play a crucial role in attempts to change societal attitudes and influence current policy and legislation. This chapter aims to explore relevant theories and concepts linked to SEND, parenting and partnership working and discuss how this knowledge can be used to strengthen collaborative working.

What Is a Theory?

Theories are used to create explanations and develop understanding; they help us to comprehend phenomena and to explain why and how, we do what we do (Cortina, 1993; Mason, 2012). A theory takes a set of identified variables (for example, the diverse forms of SEND, disparate family situations, the different professional identities of those working with families) and tries to find connections between them (for instance, do all families react in the same way to the news that their child has a special need or disability? Or, are there similarities in parental experiences?) If links are found, general assumptions can be made to form the basis of a hypothesis. This will then be tested through research and the application of prior knowledge and can form the basis of a theory which can be generalised to similar phenomena and situations (Ferris et al., 2012). While there is an argument to be made that it is hard to quantify, or make categoric assumptions about something as unpredictable as human behaviour, social theories can be used as a way to help us better understand each other and build more empathetic relationships. For those with SEND and their families, the knowledge that what they are experiencing is not unique to them, that there is an explanation, and it has a name, that it is a normal response to an abnormal situation (Roos, 2014) can be comforting and can help them to feel less isolated:

> I thought I was the only person who felt this way. It helps knowing that it has a name.
>
> (Tessa)

Theories and concepts can help to make the abstract more concrete and to find meaning in what had seemed meaningless. Knowledge of theories of disability and linked theories can potentially help us all to better understand the challenges faced by those with SEND and support the development of improved partnerships.

Disability: Key Concepts and Theories

Inclusion

Inclusion means different things to different people (Hornby, 2015) (see Chapter 3 on "The Social and the Medical Model: The Great Debate"). Theories of disability can provide frameworks of

DOI: 10.4324/9781003089506-5

support in understanding how parents and professionals can work effectively in true partnership, in order for inclusion to be possible within individual circumstances.

Ladder of Participation

Hart's Ladder of Participation (1992) defines an incremental process in which the scale and intensity of children's participation increase. The model does not require that the ladder has to be climbed sequentially, with each step having been achieved, before progressing. Instead, the stages, or "rungs of the ladder", represent increasing levels of sophistication and complexity. The bottom rungs of the ladder are characterised by passivity, reflecting the idea that "if you do something for me, without me, you do it to me". The middle part of the ladder, *"informing, consulting and engaging"*, involves working in partnership but does not include active participation. Scott considers that professional involvement should occur at a level no lower than the, *"Doing For – Engaging and Involving People"*, stage of the ladder. This should be the minimum standard of informed participation (Scott, 2021, Beaton et al., 2021). The following quote from the interviews illustrates this:

> being believed, being reassured, obviously you become an expert … I'm the expert because my child has a rare genetic condition or something, when you do have that information,……
> you need to be respected and listened to.
>
> (Caroline)

The highest rungs of the ladder, *"Doing With – Equal Partnership"*, provides an environment where active participation can take place. For professionals, this means trying to make time to really know the families they are working with; for families, this means trying to understand the pressures that professionals are under:

> try and see the parent as the person who is the professional because they are the professionals of their child. They are there with them 24/7. They know what their child is able to do what they are not able to do. So just listen to that parent, I think it is my biggest thing. I think be supportive for that parent and admit if you haven't got resources or you don't know how to find those resources. Work with that parent to do it, rather than against them.
>
> (Jules)

Labelling Theory

Identifying and distinguishing between different groups inevitably requires some form of categorisation, or labelling, to bring focus to discussion and supportive intervention. Labelling can be positive, a diagnosis may help to create a positive identity and may lead to appropriate sources of support:

> he doesn't feel the need to get a diagnosis. He doesn't think it will make a difference to his life, and I disagree and I have told him that. You know, if only for the fact that it's always nice to know who you are.
>
> (Hannah)

Conversely, labelled individuals can come to be defined by a prescribed "label", and other distinctions that make them individuals, and are key to their identity, can be overlooked (Brown, 2016, p.92):

> you know one autistic child, you know one autistic child. You don't know all autistic children. Yes, there are similar characteristics but you can't pigeon hole all of them.
>
> (Evelyn)

The problem identified, in the quote from Evelyn, is one of overgeneralisation, that a child with a diagnosis of autism will be the same as any other child with autism. Overgeneralisation of an individual's needs on the basis of a specific label is not helpful to professionals either; for example, when a teacher is attempting to provide effective learning opportunities, appropriate for the learner's individual needs. The problem with vague and inappropriate labelling in the education system is that it can allow learners to be pushed through the wrong doors from the outset. This, in turn, can create professional preconceptions that may be resistant to change (Rose & Howley, 2007; Imray & Colley, 2017, p.10). This emphasises the importance of ensuring a holistic view: listening to and "hearing" the voices of individuals and their parents/carers in the process of co-production:

> if someone's got preconceived ideas of autism and when that child doesn't meet them or particularly display what they think autism should be, they think there's no problem and that I'm being a paranoid mum.
>
> (Hannah)

> I had to try and explain my child to other people because they viewed it in a certain way.
>
> (Evelyn)

Labelling specific needs can be positive in leading individuals and their families to access networks of support and in helping to make sense of their individual experiences within commonalities of a specific label (category of need):

> I remember thinking at the time, if our daughter had Down Syndrome, we could have we could have gone every week to the Down South group and we could have talked to other parents with Down Syndrome kids... It sounds a bit ridiculous now, but then she would have got speech therapy from this lovely Speech Therapist, where, [at the time] we were getting none.
>
> (Ava)

Imray and Colley (2017) argue that avoiding identifying and labelling children with specific needs will not prevent them from being stigmatised, but it may prevent them from getting the education that they need; for example, it might limit teachers' understanding of children's difficulties and how they may best respond to them (Ayres et al., 2011; Terzi, 2010).

Contact Theory

Contact theory is informed by the idea that intergroup contact under particular conditions can reduce prejudice between majority and minority groups. While some theorists believed that contact between groups bred "suspicion, fear, resentment, disturbance, and at times open conflict" (Baker, 1934); others, such as Lett (1945), believed that intergroup contact led to "mutual understanding and regard". Applying this theory to disability, we might consider "intergroups" as representing the interaction between those who identify as disabled and wider society.

Allport (1955, cited in Katz, 1991) noted that intergroup contact can both reduce and exacerbate prejudice. This suggests that inclusion and integration between disabled people and non-disabled people may, but not always, reduce negative attitudes and presumptions and positively promote understanding. Allport adopted four "positive factors" deemed necessary for reducing prejudice within intergroup contact:

1. **Equal Status Between Groups**: Members of the contact situation should not have an unequal, hierarchical relationship (e.g. teacher/student, employer/employee).
2. **Common Goals**: Members must rely on each other to achieve their shared desired goal. To have effective contact, typically groups need to be making active effort towards a goal that the groups share.
3. **Intergroup Cooperation**: Members should work together in a non-competitive environment. According to Allport (1955), the attainment of these common goals must be based on cooperation over competition.
4. **The Support of Authorities, Law, or Custom**: The support of authorities, law and custom also tends to lead to more positive intergroup contact effects because authorities can establish norms of acceptance and guidelines for how group members should interact with each other.

From this model, we can conclude that, when those with negative attitudes towards disability find themselves in situations of positive social interactions with disabled people, their attitudes and behaviours *can* change. However, Forbes (1997) asserts that most social scientists implicitly assume that increased intergroup contact *will* reduce tensions, by giving each group information about the other, groups will thereby learn about, and from, each other (Nickerson, 2021).

Nevertheless, Allport's contact conditions leave open the question of whether contact with one group will always lead to less prejudicial opinions of other outgroups (ibid). In this example, Tessa questions whether less prejudicial opinions of disabled children will apply when those children become adults:

> it's a wider society issue because where did the kids learn? They are already learning it from their parents. They're learning it from all sorts of social cues, they're learning it from the fact that they don't see disabled people out and about. I think lots of people feel threatened... I think there's a lot of fear. I think people are often tolerant of disabled children but not disabled adults.

> (Tessa)

Maslow's Hierarchy of Needs

Abraham Harold Maslow was an American psychologist who developed a hierarchy of needs to explain human motivation. Maslow (1943) states that humans require opportunities to ensure basic needs are met in order to flourish; the highest state of flourishing being "self-actualisation". Maslow's "hierarchy of needs" is visually represented here (see Figure 4.1).

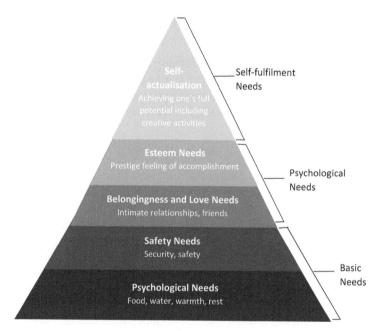

Figure 4.1 Maslow's Hierarchy of Needs.

The base of the hierarchy represents basic physiological needs: food, water, warmth, shelter and sleep. This first level of needs must be met before the next level: love and belonging can be achieved. Only when these needs are met, can self-actualisation be achieved and a sense of "morality, creativity, spontaneity, problem solving, lack of prejudice and acceptance of facts" can be developed (Spohrer, 2008, p.18).

Cameron refers us to Maslow's suggestion that, whether or not a need is met, is decided by what a community views as a priority, meaning that any idea of need is dependent on the wishes and desires of that community (2014, p.106). Cameron argues that disabled people have typically experienced marginalisation and discrimination; therefore, value is not typically attached by society to disabled peoples' needs, aspirations or even to their entitlements (ibid). For example, there has been a historic assumption that people with impairments are less able to make contributions to the workforce (Oliver, 1990). Consequently, disabled people are frequently characterised as economically inactive or unproductive (Berghs & Dyson, 2022). Therefore, the needs of disabled people are not prioritised by society because it is assumed they do not contribute to the economic wellbeing of the wider community (Barnes, 2018). These assumptions contribute to the structural oppression and marginalisation of disabled people, with a corresponding risk both to self-esteem and the likelihood of self-actualisation.

Bronfenbrenner's Ecological Theory

If Maslow's hierarchy of needs is affected by interactions within communities, the complexity of interactions can be understood within the context of Bronfenbrenner's ecological systems theory (see Figure 4.2). According to this model, children and young people's development can only be understood as embedded within and influenced by the totality of their context (Edmond & Price, 2012).

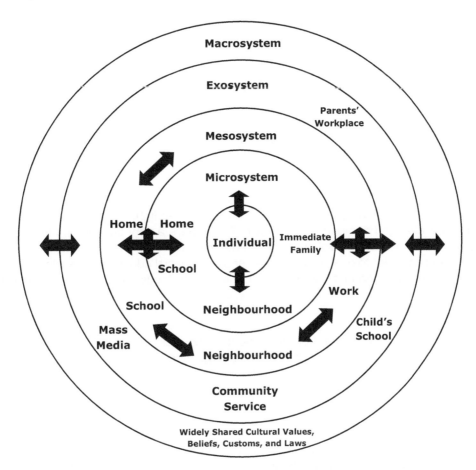

Figure 4.2 Bronfenbrenner's Ecological Model.

The concentric circles represent the individual and their family in the innermost "microsystem" and the widening circles around them represent increasingly wider "macrosystems" of society and environment. The theory considers the child's experience and understanding of the world from the middle out (Knowles, 2021, p.136). The various elements are defined as follows:

Microsystem – Activities, social roles and interpersonal relations experienced by the individual in a given face-to-face setting; for example, family, school, peer group, workplace.

Mesosystem – The linkages and processes taking place between two or more settings; for example, the relationship between home and school.

Exosystem – The linkages and processes between two or more settings, at least one of which does not contain the individual but is influenced by such settings; for example, the impact on a child and the relation between the home and the parent's workplace.

Macrosystem – The overarching cultures or subcultures, with particular reference to beliefs, bodies of knowledge, customs and life styles.

Chronosystem – The changes made over time, not just with the person individually but also of the environment in which they live. An example would be the outbreak of the global pandemic of 2019.

Applying Bronfenbrenner's ecological theory, we might consider an individual child with additional learning needs and disabilities is at the innermost "micro" circle, the heart of the model. They are embedded in families, which, in turn, interact with a series of other systems – classrooms, schools, communities and the wider society. Key factors may include:

- Family factors: their partnerships with schools, their needs for support and their involvement in parent support/partnerships.
- Classroom factors comprising strategies and adaptions to the curriculum, assessment and pedagogy, and peer support.
- School factors, which may include leadership, school culture and the deployment of human and capital resources.
- Community factors may include relationships with employers and other agencies.
- Bureaucracy, legislation and policy affecting Education, Health and Social Care sectors.
- Societal factors, including educational policies, resourcing and government accountability mechanisms.

Such systems should be "joined up", which involve both horizontal and vertical interactions. Horizontal interactions require linking systems at the same level to ensure consistency and compatibility of approach (such as among staff in a school). Vertical interactions require linking more immediate, proximal systems in which they are embedded (such as schools, communities and the wider society). Influences between systems are bi-directional. Just as families influence children, so too do children influence their families (Mitchell & Sutherland, 2020, p.71):

> What was apparent was the children who had parents who didn't have the wherewithal either financially or educationally or cognitively or emotionally to fight for their child, those children were short-changed compared to our own. And there's a very stark example of that there was a child in the Primary School speech and language class, whose mother was a single mother and had a lot to deal with besides her sons' special educational needs. For her, education just wasn't important, there were other things [to focus on]. So long as he was happy, that would be fine.
>
> (Nigel)

> my parents felt discrimination from their friends who didn't know what to say to them. But he's the life and soul and glue that keeps us all together.
>
> (Lianna)

Partnership

> Partnership involves parents, families and practitioners working together to benefit/support children. Each recognises, respects and values what the other does and says. And for me partnership means responsibility on both sides.
>
> (Lori)

Parents and other family members have critical roles in supporting learners with additional needs. They are sources of information, partners in designing and implementing programmes and advocates for their children (Mitchell & Sutherland, 2020, p.188). The notion of partnership is not new: Mittler and Mittler (1982, pp.10–11) defined partnership between parents and professionals as "a full sharing of knowledge and experience", while Pugh and De'Ath (1989, p.68) emphasised that partnership is a working relationship characterised by "a shared sense of purpose, mutual responsibility, skills, decision-making and accountability".

As Evelyn describes below, an effective partnership is a two-way process of sharing information and any concerns. What happens at home may impact on what happens in school and vice versa. Families are more likely to share information if they feel equally valued in the partnership of meeting their child's full individual needs (Knowles, 2021).

> My knowledge of special needs is how they present in school, how they affect the way they work in school. You don't have the knowledge of what goes on at home, or how it affects them at home and a lot of times it's very different.
>
> (Evelyn)

Person-Centred/Child-Centred Approach

Person-centred (and child-centred) approaches place the person/child and their family as the "expert"; as the main source of "knowledge", in order to understand the individual's strengths, interests, preferences, challenges and to share future aspirations (Martin-Denham & Watts, 2019).

Article 12 of the UNCRC (1989) advocates a child's right to participate in decisions that are made about their lives and to have their voice heard. It also states that adults must assist children to have their views, feelings and aspirations placed at the centre of future plans. This approach is the main principle of the SEND Code of Practice: 0–25 (2015): "A person-centred approach is where the views of children and caregivers are taken into account when decisions are made" (DfE, 2015, p.245).

Having this approach incorporated within legislation and policy ensures that professionals are required to make provision to elicit the voices of the child/young person and their family. It places an emphasis on the ethical imperative that professionals must work together for the best interests of the child, even if this presents challenges for the professional (Hellawell, 2019).

> You know, the idea that you have a diagnosis in front of you does not make you know the person that you are reading about. Sometimes getting to know people it's more than one dimensional, it's not just that paperwork, it is the individuals behind the person as well.
>
> (Robert)

> What you see as a teacher of a child with SEND, is nothing in comparison to what you see as a parent and the child with SEND.
>
> (Evelyn)

Robert and Evelyn provide validation of the importance of placing the power of expertise with the child/young person and their families as authentic sources of knowledge.

Collaboration

Collaboration can be defined as a process that enables groups of people with diverse expertise to combine their resources to generate solutions to problems (Mitchell & Sutherland, 2020). Nevertheless, collaboration can be a nebulous concept:

> ..we all get along, we co-operate, discuss and share resources; we work side by side, help each other out, and support each other. We work together on committees, sports teams and special events. We're very collaborative…. Aren't we?
>
> (Sharratt & Planche, 2016)

This quote may describe a collegiate environment; however, is collaboration simply about "getting along" and "supporting each other"? In some cases, "getting along" and "supporting each other" may easily lead to maintaining the current status quo. If collaboration is to be purposeful then it must also include "challenge" (Thompson & Spenceley, 2020, p.74).

Co-production

Co-production relates to the strategic direction of planning and outcome for people who use a range of services. Swain et al. (2014, p.230) describe co-production as a way of creative thinking, designing, delivering, monitoring and evaluating services in an equal relationship between staff, people who use services, and their families, friends and neighbours. True co-production relies on professionals and people who are in receipt of services working together in a collaborative way, but it can be difficult to achieve. In response to questions from the authors, both professionals and parents cite the lack of time as a potential challenge in working collaboratively together. It could also be argued, that co-production is a feeling, an emotional response to successful collaboration involving mutual respect. If this is the case, then even the best efforts of allowing time and space for co-production to take place, may not be enough:

> It is not just about parents, it needs to start with the professionals to understand what [co-production] is and what it should look and feel like because it's not just a process, it's a feeling. I think it won't be for everyone because people are human and working together, participation is not for everyone. That's okay. But it just helps keep you going a bit longer

otherwise you end up burning yourself out by going against the system all the time and feeling like you're not being heard and that's because most people aren't heard.

(Lianna)

Parenting a Child with SEND: Key Theories

Attachment Theory

Attachment describes a bond based on affection between two people. When a child is securely attached, they feel a sense of emotional security and comfort in the presence of their parent or primary caregiver. As children grow and develop, they use this attachment to act as a secure base for exploration and development, allowing them to gain a sense of self and independence (Bee & Boyd, 2013). For children with SEND, the attachment to their parents can often be part of a lifelong inter-dependency where parents feel as though their child will not be able to flourish without them and children do not feel emotionally safe if their parents are not present:

> I just developed this connection with him. I just… he wouldn't smile at anyone because he's obviously in pain the whole time and so he had this really serious look on his face all the time, they said he never smiled, he never smiles but when I came along he just broke into this smile and then everyone just cheered and I just… we just suddenly had this really strong connection and.. that was it really,
>
> (Mathew)

> he's going to go off and then he's there without you and he's so vulnerable,
>
> (Lianna)

Key pioneers in the study of attachment were Mary Ainsworth and John Bowlby. While Ainsworth studied the impact of different forms of attachment (Ainsworth, 1969a), Bowlby (1958) explored the emotional impact of secure attachment (or lack of secure attachment) on children, positing that healthy attachments are important for a child's survival. He believed that children need to experience "warm, intimate and continuous relationships with their mother" or primary caregiver and that to not have this could cause irrevocable damage to their mental health.

For parents, the shock of learning that their child has a special need or waiting for a diagnosis can sometimes cause an initial barrier to bonding:

> I'm not sure I really connected with him He was such a beautiful baby, I looked after and I cared for him but I think, because they lost the blood sample, it took 8 days to get an official diagnosis. So, I think because I was in limbo in that stage it kind of, prevented me from connecting with him as much as I could have
>
> (Larissa)

> it took a few months; but, at some point, something switched on I just thought "right okay I've got to do the best I can for this child" and as she developed, she was a delight actually you know…. in a way, when she's not being the stroppy teenager she still is now
>
> (Tessa)

However, once the barriers are broken down, the parent/child relationship often becomes one of ferocious love, where parents feel that they must constantly do battle, becoming "warrior parents" (Lamb, 2009, p.2): fighting the system, societal attitudes and embedded prejudice to ensure that the rights of their child are met.

For those with SEND, the initial developmental step of moving away from their parent or caregiver, both physically and emotionally, does not occur in the same way as it does for other children and young adults. Consequently, throughout their lives, the parents will continue to be the secure base that is returned to (Bee & Boyd, 2013). Unlike other parents, their children may never leave home or live independently. The attachment is linked to the continual awareness of the "*phenomenal vulnerability*" (Ava) of their children and becomes defined by their lifelong role as an advocate and protector:

> The only person on this earth who truly cares enough about my child to fight for him, is me.
>
> (Catherine)

While the intensity of the attachment experienced by most parents during the first 2 years of their child's life lessens as their children grow (Bowlby & Ainsworth, 2013), for parents of children with SEND, it can deepen as they watch their children struggle to achieve what comes naturally to others. The depth of attachment is linked to a fear of the future, of what will happen to their child when they die. This is part of the concept of chronic sorrow:

> one of the worst things of having a disabled child, is thinking about time and the future, and what happens when we are around and that's something that haunts me, terrifies me.
>
> (Jonno)

> he is a constant joy. It's just, it's just that fear of the future and that he is so vulnerable. You hear terrible things about care homes and everything else.
>
> (Susan)

Chronic Sorrow

Chronic sorrow (Olshansky, 1962) is a hidden sorrow, experienced specifically by parents of children with SEND and those caring for people with chronic illnesses. It typically begins at birth or diagnosis. The genesis of the sadness is the recognition of the loss of the hoped-for child and of the reality of the life their child will be living, compared to the future the parent had dreamt of. Chronic sorrow is described by Roos (2014) as a "living loss" and by Busch (2013) as a sorrow that is both ongoing and cyclical. It is lifelong and is re-experienced every time a child fails to meet a milestone, for example, walking, talking, passing a driving test and leaving home. It is estimated that 80% of parents of children with SEND experience chronic sorrow (Boss et al., 2021). The fact that chronic sorrow is interwoven with periods of satisfaction and happiness (Teel, 2013) means that it is sometimes unrecognised and can be overlooked by professionals as a cause of parental anxiety:

> it is the chronic sorrow bit and I think it almost gets worse as they get older. I can see maybe what her life could be and all the things she's not going to be able to do…. that is the worst bit of it.
>
> (Tessa)

Emotional Labour

Emotional labour is a term coined by Hochschild (1983) and described as: "The effort within oneself to conjure appropriate feelings or subdue inappropriate ones, and the effort to induce particular feelings in another person or stifle other feelings" (Mastracci et al., 2011, p.28).

Initially, Hochschild distinguished between "commodified" emotional labour, within the workplace, and "emotion work" within the domestic sphere. However, the terms are frequently used interchangeably.

Emotional labour is unpaid emotional "work": it is the work parents do to comfort, support and protect their children, helping them to be resilient and positive while disguising their own fears and worries. Emotional labour demands a constant reappraisal, comparison and analysis of affective states to ensure that the right action is taken (Mastracci et al., 2011); for parents, this action will often be to protect their children. For most parents, the main burden of emotional work lessens as their children get older; for parents of children with SEND this is not the case; they must often continue to labour emotionally for their children throughout their lives. This can lead to burnout and emotional exhaustion (Gérain & Zech, 2018; Davenport & Zolnikov, 2021).

Parents are often unaware of the physical and emotional impact of emotional labour, believing it to be integral to their role as parent and protector; this means that it often goes unrecognised by professionals, and parents do not ask for support (Dyson, 2004):

> I'm exhausted by the working, I'm exhausted by it all …. … I just can't think of a way out really… it's not going to stop is it? It's just going to go on and on and I'm 63 and I'm really tired.
>
> (Matthew)

Containment Theory

The theory of containment was developed by Bion in 1963. Heavily influenced by the work of Melanie Klein, Bion used the image of a mother and breast-feeding child to explain the concept. Based on the idea that a baby is vulnerable and defenceless and unable to manage their intrinsic fear, Bion posited that their anxieties are contained by their mother. Effective containment is made up of two elements, the container and the contained. The baby (the contained) transfers his or her fears to the mother, (the container) who is able to process and filter them, returning them in a more manageable form thereby calming and comforting the baby (Sandler, 2013).

The theory of containment is linked to SEND in two ways:

- The constant containing of their children's emotions is an ongoing state for parents and carers and is linked to emotions. While other children will gradually reduce their dependence on parental emotional containment, transferring this role to friends and later partners, parents of children with SEND often remain the permanent container of anxieties and fears.
- The parents and carers themselves often lack someone to be their "container". Referring to Bronfenbrenner's ecological systems theory (see above), it can be seen that, in families with a child with SEND, the microsystem is often small. Parents report feeling isolated and separated from parents who do not have a child with a SEN or disability who cannot, therefore, understand their experience. Ava remembers being in a group where someone was discussing the unreasonable demands made by parents of children with SEND:

> (the other group member said) 'And do you know, there are all these parents who want their children to go to these schools that, you know, cost like 10 times what the local provision costs, and you know they all think that their children should get everything.' It was really funny, because half the class knew, … I think it might have even been just the time that we were fighting with them and I could see all the other people in the class all going 'ooooh,' and then I just said to her, 'you know, I'm one of those parents. What would you do if you knew what your child needed… what would you do?'
>
> (Ava)

The emotions evoked by this continual sense of otherness, added to the emotional exhaustion of parenthood, the impact of chronic sorrow, concerns for the future and a perception of being in a constant battle with an inflexible, system, can lead to emotional burnout (Gérain & Zech, 2018; Davenport & Zolnikov, 2021). Without containment themselves, parents are unable to act as containers for their children, this can result in an escalation of challenging behaviours, consequent feelings of guilt that they are "bad" parents and periods of heightened anxiety for the whole family. Recognising signs of emotional overload, identifying someone to act transactionally as a "container", understanding that being a "good enough", parent (Winnicott, 1957) is good enough and developing strategies to support the development of resilience can help to prevent adverse reactions:

> there are those moments where you might be just reaching the end of your tether and you can almost tag out and we've got better at reading that and sort of, 'you know I'll go and deal with this,' or vice versa, just to balance it out because the other thing with our son is, well there's no point getting really het up and angry as if you elevate he's just going to elevate more you know, and you can't come back from that.
>
> (Hope)

Knowledge and understanding of theory allow parents and practitioners to make sense of what is happening and to work together to mitigate against worse case scenarios. Sometimes knowing what a theory is, can make a real difference.

Key Take-Aways

- Theories of disability can provide frameworks of support in understanding the challenges faced by those with SEND.

- Active participation can occur when professionals make time to really know the families they are working with, and families understand the pressures professionals are under.
- Labelling affords opportunities towards creating a positive identity and to appropriate sources of support. However, "labelled" individuals can have aspects of their individuality and identity overlooked.
- Contact theory is the idea that positive social interactions with disabled people can change attitudes towards disability.
- Parents and other family members are more likely to share critical information if they feel equally valued in the partnership.

Topics for Discussion

1. How might attitudes and behaviours create a disabling environment?
2. Person-centred approaches place the person/child and their family as the "expert". Do you agree/disagree, and why?
3. Which of the theories and concepts discussed in this chapter do you find the most compelling? Does your view change depending on whether you argue as a disabled person, as a parent/family member or as a professional?

References

Ainsworth, M. D. S. (1969a) The effects of maternal deprivation: A review of findings and controversy in the context of research strategy. In: *Deprivation of Maternal Care: A Reassessment of Its Effects. Public Health Papers*, 14. Geneva: World Health Organization, pp. 97–165

Ainsworth, M. D. S. (1969b) Object relationships, dependency, and attachment: A theoretical review of the infant-mother relationship. *Child Development*, 40, 969–1026.

Ayres, K. M., Lowery, K. A., Douglas, K. H., & Sievers, C. (2011) I can identify Saturn but I can't brush my teeth: What happens when the curricular focus for students with severe disabilities shifts. *Education and Training in Autism and Developmental Disabilities*, 46, 11–21.

Baker, P. E. (1934) Negro-white adjustment in America. *Journal of Negro Education*, 3, 194–204.

Barnes, C. (2018) Theories of disability and the origins of the oppression of disabled people in western society. In *Disability and Society*. London: Routledge, pp. 43–60.

Bee & Boyd, D. (2013) The developing child. *Singapore Journal of Education*, 37, 2014.

Berghs, M., & Dyson, S. M. (2022) Intersectionality and employment in the United Kingdom: Where are all the Black disabled people? *Disability & Society*, 37(4), 543–566.

Boss, P., Roos, S., & Harris, D. L. (2021) Grief in the midst of ambiguity and uncertainty: An exploration of ambiguous loss and chronic sorrow. In R. A. Neimeyer, D. L. Harris, H. R. Winokuer & G. F. Thornton (eds.) *Grief and Bereavement in Contemporary Society*. London: Routledge, pp. 163–175.

Bowlby, J. (1958) The nature of the child's tie to his mother. *International Journal of Psychoanalysis*, 39, 350–371.

Bowlby, J., & Ainsworth, M. (2013) The origins of attachment theory. *Attachment Theory: Social, Developmental, and Clinical Perspectives*, 45(28), 759–775.

Brown, Z. (2016) *Inclusive Education: Perspectives on Pedagogy, Policy and Practice*. Oxon: Routledge.

Busch, S. (2013) Chronic sorrow. Available at: https://susanellisonbusch.com/chronic-sorrow-in-parenting-a-child-with-a-disability/ (Accessed 1 September 2022)

Cameron, C. (2014) *Disability Studies: A Student's Guide*. London: Sage.

Cortina, J. M. (1993) What is co-efficient alpha? An examination of theory and applications. *Journal of Applied Psychology*, 78(1), 98.

Davenport, S., & Zolnikov, T. R. (2021) Understanding mental health outcomes related to compassion fatigue in parents of children diagnosed with intellectual disability. *Journal of Intellectual Disabilities*, 17446295211013600.

Department for Education (DfE). (2015) *Special Educational Needs and Disability Code of Practice: 0–25 Years*. London: DfE.

Dyson, S. (2004) *Mental Handicap Dilemmas of Parent-Professional Relations*. New York: Croom Helm.

Edmond, N., & Price, M. (2012) *Integrated Working with Children and Young People: Supporting Development from Birth to Nineteen*. London: Sage.

Ferris, G.R., Hochwarter, W.A. & Buckley, M.R., (2012) Theory in the organizational sciences: How will we know it when we see it? *Organizational Psychology Review*, 2(1), 94–106.

Forbes, H. (1997) *Ethnic Conflict, Commerce, Culture and the Contact Hypothesis*. London: University Press.

Gérain, P., & Zech, E. (2018) Does informal caregiving lead to parental burnout? Comparing parents having (or not) children with mental and physical issues. *Frontiers in Psychology*, 9, 884.

Hellawell, B. (2019) *Understanding and Challenging the SEND Code of Practice*. London: Sage.

Hochschild, A. (1983) *The Managed Heart: Commercialization of Human Feeling.* Berkeley: University of California Press.

Hornby, G. (2015) Inclusive special education: Development of a new theory for the education of children with special educational needs and disabilities. *British Journal of Special Education*, 42(3), 234–256.

Imray, P., & Colley, A. (2017) *Inclusion is Dead: Long Live Inclusion*. Oxon: Routledge.

Katz, I. (1991) Gordon Allport's "The Nature of Prejudice." *Political Psychology*, 12(1), 125–157. https://doi.org/10.2307/3791349

Knowles, G. (2021) Working with families. In Beaton, M., Codina, G., & Wharton, J. (eds.) *Leading on Inclusion: The Role of the SENCO*. Oxon: Routledge, pp. 131–139.

Lamb, B. (2009) *Lamb Inquiry, Special Educational Needs and Parental Confidence*. London: DCFS.

Lett, H. A. (1945) Techniques for achieving interracial cooperation. *Harvard Educational Review*, 15(1), 62–71.

Martin-Denham, S., & Watts, S. (2019) *The SENCO Handbook: Leading Provision and Practice*. California: Corwin.

Maslow, A. H. (1943) A theory of human motivation. *Psychological Review*, 50(4), 370–396.

Mason, R. (2012) *Understanding Understanding*. New York: SUNY Press.

Mastracci, S. H., et al. (2011) *Emotional Labor and Crisis Response: Working on the Razor's Edge*. Routledge. ProQuest Ebook Central. Available at: https://ebookcentral.proquest.com/lib/chiuni-ebooks/detail.action?docID=1900134.

Mitchell, D., & Sutherland, D. (2020) *What Really Works in Special and Inclusive Education: Using Evidence-Based Teaching Strategies*. Oxon: Routledge.

Mittler, P., & Mittler, H. (1982) *Partnership with Parents*. Stratford-upon-Avon: National Council for Special Education.

Nickerson, C. (2021, November 01) *Allport's Intergroup Contact Hypothesis: Its History and Influence*. Simply Psychology. Available at: www.simplypsychology.org/contact-hypothesis.html (Accessed 30 August 2022).

Oliver, M. (1990) Critical texts in social work and the welfare state the politics of disablement. *Recuperado de*. Available at: https://disability-studies.leeds.ac.uk/library.

Olshansky, S. (1962) Chronic sorrow: a response to having a mentally defective child. *Social casework*, 43(4), 190–193.

Pugh, G., & De'Ath, E. (1989) *Working Towards Partnership in the Early Years*. London: National Children's Bureau.

Roos, S. (2014) *Chronic Sorrow: A Living Loss*. London: Routledge.

Rose, R., & Howley, M. (2007) *The Practical Guide to Special Educational Needs in Inclusive Primary Classrooms*. London: Sage.

Sandler, P. C. (2013) *A Clinical Application of Bion's Concepts: Free associations and free-floating attention*. London: Routledge.

Scott, A. (2021) Person-centred approaches. In Beaton, M., Codina, G., & Wharton, J. (eds.) *Leading on Inclusion: The Role of the SENCO*. Oxon: Routledge, pp. 91–98.

Sharratt, L. D., & Planche, B. M. (2016) *Leading Collaborative Learning: Empowering Excellence*. London: Sage.

Spohrer, K. (2008) *Teaching Assistant's Guide to Emotional and Behavioural Difficulties*. London: Continuum.

Swain, J., French, S., Barnes, C., & Thomas, C. (2014) *Disabling Barriers – Enabling Environments*. London: Sage.

Teel, C. (2013) *Chronic Sorrow: Analysis of the Concept*. Available at: https://onlinelibrary.wiley.com/doi/pdf/10.1111/j.1365-2648.1991.tb01559.x# (Accessed 20 July 2022)

Terzi, L. (2010) *Justice and Equality in Education: A Capability Perspective on Disability and Special Educational Needs*. London: Continuum.

Thompson, C., & Spenceley, L. (2020) *Learning Theories for Everyday Teaching*. London: Sage.

Winnicott, D. W. (1957) *Mother and Child: A Primer of First Relationships.* New York: Basic Books.

5 Making Co-production Work

Introduction

Co-production was enshrined in law for those with SEND (special educational needs and disability) through the Children and Families Act (2014) and the Care Act (2014). Designed to ensure that decisions about their services and resources are made by, for and (most importantly) with service users, effective co-production is an essential building block to the creation of true partnerships between professionals and those with SEND and their families. This chapter will explore what is meant by co-production and why it can be hard to embed; how it differs from multi-agency working, potential benefits and how to ensure that those with SEND and their families have a voice and that they remain at the heart of any decisions made about them.

Partnership Working

> Partnership involves parents, families and practitioners working together to benefit/support children. Each recognises, respects and values what the other does and says. And for me partnership means responsibility on both sides.
>
> (Lori)

The concept of partnership, in relation to working with parents of children with SEND, is subjective and open to (mis)interpretation. According to Ryan and Runswicke-Cole (2008), the term partnership is often loosely understood by professionals as a model of involvement; rather than a true partnership which supports the rights of the parents to make decisions about their children (Green & Edwards, 2021).

The "discourse of shared decision-making" (Cribb & Gerwitz, 2012, p.508) relates to ideas of choice, pupil and parent voice, personalisation and co-production. In some instances, the shared "decision-making" involves the "participation" of individuals where they are invited and enabled to express their views and take part in debates:

> For me, it is about building a **partnership** with professionals. We all want to work together for the benefit of the child. We all want to support the child throughout his journey, care or school environments.
>
> (Lori)

An alternative to or an extension of partnership working is one of co-production, where everyone involved, including those with disabilities and their families, have to agree on desired outcomes together and recommendations and actions are produced collectively.

What Is Co-production?

The concept of co-production is linked to the idea of person-centred planning, which puts the individual at the heart of processes and decisions made about them. Described by Boyle and

DOI: 10.4324/9781003089506-6

Harris (2009) as a way to deliver public services by creating "an equal and reciprocal relationship between professionals, people using services, (and) their families", it is designed to ensure that the views of the service users themselves form the basis for service design and delivery. It reflects the motto of the Union of the Physically Impaired Against Segregation (UPIAS), "nothing about us without us" (1972), and for those with SEND, the legislative legitimacy co-production has been given in the Children and Families Act (2014) and the Care Act (2014), represents the triumph of the social model of disability over the medical model.

At its best, co-production should foster equal partnerships between service providers and service users, forcing all involved to consider and effectively challenge the underlying causes of inequality and to create user-led strategies based on aspirational individual need (Boyle and Harris, 2009). Successful co-production recognises and values different forms of knowledge and skills and is based on the understanding that everyone, who is part of the process, has something worthwhile and valuable to contribute (Boyle and Harris, 2009). By including those with SEND and their families, the co-productive process creates agency; a sense of being in control, for participants allowing agreed, shared targets and outcomes to be personal, appropriate and aspirational (Green & Edwards, 2021).

In 2007, the Prime Minister, David Cameron, described co-production as a way to move service users from being "passive recipients of state services" to "active doers of their own life". Yet despite a political, legal and ethical consensus that co-production should be embedded at all levels of planning and provision, there is still no clear understanding of what co-production should entail and importantly what co-produced services should look like (Brandsen et al., 2018). Co-production represents a changing approach to decision-making, rather than a prescriptive method (INVOLVE, 2016):

> it's not just a process, it's a feeling…..? I think you've got to experience it and every practitioner professional needs to know what it should look and feel like

> (Lianna)

Changing Perceptions: Embedding Co-production in Practice

Change, whether personal or professional, is often perceived as a threat, evoking feelings of fear, anxiety and loss of control (Forrest, 2013). This is especially true in the workplace, where change can be perceived as a threat to competence and professional identity (Forrest, 2013). This anxiety and unwillingness to change is sensed by parents, often leading to feelings of frustration and disempowerment:

> people who have been in the profession for quite a long time are quite resistant… they think they know how to do it and think.., 'we've Individual, group and organisational. As such it impacts the structure, creation and delivery of services from Education, Health and Care Plan (EHCP) meetings to strategic financial planning. Such a cultural shift can take time to be accepted and embedded in practice, with complete conceptual integration and changed attitudes only occurring with investment in effective grassroots training and ongoing professional development.

> I've always been quite.. happy to engage with… the younger person who's not the experienced person…Like (our daughter's) SENCO at her old school. It was really great in all sorts of ways and I remember saying to her once, 'how long have you been doing this is?' and she said, 'oh well I only started in September. The old SENCO left and I did the training.' It was … because she really wanted to do it and she was really open to discussion. She wanted to learn and was finding her way, so was really open to engaging…' she would be like, 'I've had this idea, what do you think? Do you think this would work? Do you want to try it and see?'

> (Tessa)

In this way both those taking the lead in frontline delivery and those newly entering the profession have a full understanding of the importance, benefits and challenges of co-production.

While its introduction as a decision-making process depends on organisational change, its successful implementation depends on the attitudes of the individuals involved in its delivery. Both professionals and parents appreciate how difficult this can be:

> So perhaps the 'how' … does involve that kind of interpersonal dimension, but also.. that strategic dimension too.. that you have to be….an agent of change within your institutional context, and that's a big ask, I realise that. So you do need to find people who have some kind of vision or are prepared to take risks and challenge and try new things and show some leadership, and that will involve at times, coming into confrontation with the systems and institutional structures and the political structures… I think in many cases that is really problematic.
>
> (Jono)

Tokenism or Participation?

In order for professionals to be the agents for change in partnership working, it is important to understand the difference between consultation, engagement and participation. While co-production represents partnership working at its most effective, there is a risk, that, rather than listening and responding to the views of those with SEND, and their families, organisations simply use the process to extract relevant information (Groundwater-Smith & Mockler, 2016; Tisdall, 2017) in compliance with legal expectations; rather than making use of the transformational potential of true and equal participation to inform strategies and outcomes (Hall, 2017). Adapted from Hart's Ladder of Participation (1997), the image below shows the stages of engagement which lead to co-production (Figure 5.1).

The bottom rungs of the ladder represent the passive model of participation. At this stage, families and those with SEND are educated and informed of the decisions made about them; but, their views are neither sought nor included.

> we were being told that this is now what would happen, and this is how the process goes. We were not empowered to be parents at that moment.
>
> (Robert)

The middle part of the ladder includes consulting and engaging as a form of working in partnership but does not engender active participation. At this stage, service users are heard but

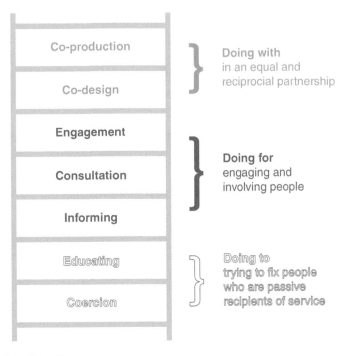

Figure 5.1 Ladder of participation.

not listened to (Cline & Frederickson, 2009) their views are asked for and they may be included in meetings and discussions; but their presence is often tokenistic, rather than participatory (Kilkelly et al., 2005). It is at this stage that training and professional development are essential, to avoid all involved getting stuck on the middle rungs of the ladder. Without a clear, shared understanding of what a co-productive approach involves, consultation – asking participants to express their views, and engagement – making sure that those with SEND and their families are in the room, can be confused with active participation:

> don't just hear it, listen to it. There's a difference.
>
> (Hannah)

Reaching the highest rungs of the ladder, providing an environment where active participation can take place, involves time and effort from all involved. Successful partnership working demands mutual respect and empathy (Boswell & Woods, 2021) and is based on an understanding that everyone has the right to participate equally whatever their needs or abilities. For professionals, this means seeing the child or adult not the disability:

> the idea that you have a diagnosis in front of you does not make you know the person that you're reading about.... our children are people. They are people with aspirations and sometimes they need... support
>
> (Robert)

For parents, this means trying to understand the pressure that professionals are under with large case loads and limited budgets.
For professionals, this means trying to make time to really know the families they are working with. For families, this means trying to understand the pressures that professionals are under. Successfully reaching the top rungs of any ladder of participation depends on the development of a trusting and honest relationship, which demands time, patience and conviction and the flexibility to learn from each other (Boswell & Woods, 2021).

> Listening is not easy, in fact its really, really difficult.. ... because you have to have some kind of conviction and you have to trust your judgement... I think listening takes time ..., you have to be prepared to make time and to understand what it is that you're listening to... That includes not understanding and not being frightened of not understanding and acknowledging that it might take time to understand. So you do have to try and let go of your own kind of professional identity at some time.
>
> (Jono)

Reaching the top of the participatory ladder by developing co-created and co-produced outcomes challenges traditional relationships between service users and service providers. This depends upon its holistic conceptual acceptance at every stage of the process and at every level of engagement; individual, organisational and multi-agency (Boswell and Woods, 2021).

Differentiating Between Co-production and Multi-Agency Working

The concepts of co-production and multi-agency working are sometimes confused in the discussion of partnership working. Multi-agency working demands collaboration between professionals, while co-production is a collaborative process involving families and service users. Both are key concepts in education and care services and one does not replace the other but they should dovetail to ensure that messages are consistent and cross-departmental services are joined up. This demands inter-disciplinary collaboration, as well as co-production, ensuring that multi-agency decisions are based on the views and needs of individual service users. Without joined-up working between professionals, parents may receive contradictory messages and feel as though they are being shuttled between departments and agencies:

> you end up being pushed from pillar to post (between) these people, who overlap massively in what they do and they all sit in different departments in different places, under different organisational structures, and accessing them all individually is an impossible task.
>
> (Jono)

Although the idea of professionals working collaboratively has informed education, health and care support in the UK since the 1970s (Warnock Report, 1979), the Laming Inquiry (2003) into the death of 8-year-old Victoria Climbie brought the importance of effective multi-agency working into stark reality. Laming was clear in his Report, that lack of multi-agency working and inter-agency working had a key role to play in Victoria's death (Laming Inquiry, 2003).

The Inquiry culminated in the 2004 Children Act, requiring local authorities to ensure effective multi-agency working between different departments and professions and to put children and families at the heart of all processes through Every Child Matters agenda (2003). This heralded the beginning of the journey towards co-production.

The Benefits of Effective Partnership Working and Co-production

Despite the investment in time and effort necessary to develop successful co-productive partnerships, it is widely acknowledged that the multiple benefits to individuals and professionals justify the extra work (Williams et al., 2010; Fern, 2014) leading to improved outcomes for those with SEND.

Benefits of Co-Production

Being Heard

Most importantly for families and service users is that co-production ensures that their voice is heard and they feel listened to:

> I can't tell you how important that is …because once someone feels that they've been heard, that takes 50% of their anxiety away.
>
> (Hannah)

This generates agency and strengthens the internal locus of control (Rotter, 1966) leading to a deconstruction of the personal tragedy theory (Oliver, 1986). Thus perceptions of those with SEND are changed from viewing them as helpless victims worthy of pity or "bundles of need" (Boyle and Harris, 2009) to seeing them as active participants in society and agents of their own outcomes. This is especially true for their families:

> They got us very involved actually, and listened to everything we had to say. They were wonderful people, it really was a partnership.
>
> (Hannah)

Empowerment

The understanding that parents know their children best and that this knowledge elevates them to the role of expert, raises their acknowledged status within the professional/parent relationship and inspires confidence that their views will be heard and valued (Cheminais, 2011; Nutbrown et al., 2009, Dyson et al, 2004):

> try and see the parent as the person who is the expert because they are with them 24/7. They know what their child is able to do what they are not able to do.
>
> (Jono)

This represents a cultural shift within organisations, where the professionals transition from being fixers of problems to facilitators of shared solutions (Boyle and Harris, 2009; Realpe & Wallace, 2010). Importantly, parents and those with SEND transition from being passive recipients to empowered decision-makers. This represents the empowerment model of partnership working (Appleton & Minchom, 1991).

Development of Positive Relationships

Effective co-production allows everyone to participate on equal terms; leading to improved relationships between professionals and service users. Co-productive relationships are based on mutual respect and empathy which enhances understanding of the impact of decisions made and pressures experienced by parents, professionals and service users (Cahn, 2000). Improved relationships and shared ownership of decisions lead to improved outcomes (Boyle and Harris, 2009).

Challenges of Co-production

The Need for Cultural Change

In order to be effective, co-production demands cultural change at organisational, group and individual levels. Roles must be re-defined and strategies must be put in place to ensure that the views of all participants are given equal value. Not just those who are more able, articulate or socially advantaged (Boyle and Harris, 2009). If this is not done, there is a risk of a two-tier system:

> the children who had parents who didn't have the wherewithal either financially or educationally or cognitively or emotionally to fight for their child, those children were short-changed.

> (Nigel)

This takes time, patience and investment in training and professional development by employers.

Lack of Shared Understanding of Terminology

Lack of clarity as to the meaning and agreed process of co-production can lead to confusion, mixed messages and differing expectations (Brandsen et al., 2018). At a group level, the use of jargon or unexplained acronyms can make it more difficult for parents and those with SEND to understand what is being discussed.

> Keep things accessible and easy.....put things in layman's terms
> (Dana)

Time

The creation of true partnerships through effective co-production takes time. It demands active listening skills, the development of trusting relationships, the creation of emotionally safe spaces and enough time in meetings to ensure that those who are less confident or less able to communicate, have time to express their views. While heavy workloads often mean that professionals are time-pressured, emotional and physical investment in effective co-production can improve outcomes and develop agency in service users; resulting in less dependency and, therefore, less pressure on services in the future (Williams et al., 2010; Fern, 2014; Boswell & Woods, 2021).

What Parents Want

Parents want to:

> Feel valued and respected.
> Be more involved in their child's journey (learning and development)
> Feel comfortable to share information
> Have confidence in their skills
> Have confidence in their abilities to support their child
> Know that their need for help to support their child is recognised to support the child
> Gain information on the service and how the service can support the child
> Make sure their voice heard.
> Make sure that the professionals recognise their expertise.

> (Lori)

The introduction of EHCPs in the Children and Families Act (2014) is underpinned by the person-centred, co-production agenda; ensuring that parental views play a crucial part in the decision-making process for her son, while the use of the graduated approach ensures that Lori's views are valued and included.

Educational, Health and Care Plans (EHCPs)

An aim of the SEND Reforms of 2014 was to ensure that the way we support children and young people is aspirational about their future (Arnold & Hoskin, 2021). The EHCP replaced the Statement of Special Educational Needs under the Children and Families Act 2014. The intention of the EHCP was to provide statutory protection, for those with additional learning needs who would require educational provision that is additional to, or different from, that which is typically offered (Sewell & Smith, 2021). A needs assessment must be conducted by the local authority (LA) in order to determine eligibility of an EHCP (Arnold & Hoskin, 2021). The right to request a needs assessment for an EHCP is held by the parent of a child, a young person (aged 16–25) or a professional from a school or college.

The "needs assessment" of eligibility for an EHCP relies on the same universal legal test as to whether an EHCP is required, with the opportunity for the LA to decline after consideration (Hellawell, 2019). Hellawell (2019) suggests that LAs may develop criteria designed to help decide if an assessment is necessary; thereby leaving an area of potential dispute between parents and local professionals wide open to local variance and possible conflict. However, as one parent describes below, the creation of meaningful and functional outcomes rely on mutual trust, placing the child or young person at the centre of any decision-making process.

> I should be able to trust the professionals and I should be honest with them (Whilst they should be honest with me) And don't forget the professionals are accountable to us! They owe us the truth as well. Actually, they are also service providers so that is another reason why they are accountable.

> (Lori)

The focus of the EHCP is placed on "outcomes", defined as "the difference or benefit made" (CoP, 9.66) to individuals. Outcomes are conceived as measurable positive consequences for the child or young person, as a result of the interventions and provisions made by professionals. These outcomes are documented in Section E of the EHCP and need to be co-produced with families. If the documented outcomes are to be aspirational, ensuring the child or young person receives positive consequences from having an EHCP, it could be argued that physically meeting the child or young person is fundamental. Susan describes her experience of contributing to her child's EHCP, outlining the positive aspect of documenting what her son can achieve. She also suggests how documenting a person's life without actually meeting them can be problematic.

Writing the EHCP there was a big rush at the end, with almost no staff left [at the local authority] to get into an EHCP. But I like nothing more than writing about my son so I really enjoyed writing that, and it felt better than writing a statement because it wasn't problem focused, it is, it's a lot more about with him. And I guess as a document it's that and it is also in the sense of I'm overly positive about Thomas and the things he can do. I might be writing about the things that are just emerging, he is getting a lot more speech since lockdown and that kind of thing and actually whether that would probably give a first impression of false positiveness in the sense of yeah I...., I don't....... **I think it's just the best thing people can do is meet them**.... obviously the people who you deal with at County are probably never going to meet your child.

(Susan)

An emphasis on "trust" in the process of co-production in producing an effective EHCP is suggested here by a parent. It could be argued to ensure EHCPs are effective, equality of knowledge and expertise from the child/young person, families and professionals is fundamental. As considered by the parent below, without authentic co-production, there is the danger of the EHCP becoming a tokenistic "paper" that meets administrative criteria only.

without the help of other people these are not really useful papers. But it is when you are then helped to see how the supportive infrastructure works with the EHCP, that's when... it then really works.

(Robert)

Robert (parent) goes on to describe the complexity of co-production in terms of equity of knowledge. This suggests that the process of compiling an effective EHCP relies on an equitable level of knowledge from the families and professionals involved.

But the thing that I don't really like about the EHCPs is that I can request everything that I need because of the knowledge that I have of the processes. But most of the parents that are [not] like me, or that were like me in the beginning, have nothing to go on. And some of them were even worse off, as this is where the Local Authorities stand proud of the fact that parents have EHCPs but they also hide behind the fact that these parents have got no way of actually understanding what they can get support in, if you know what I mean. Like okay, you need help with your child who is in social care, this help is from social care sector and this help is from education, this help is from the NHS etc. So, I think this is where the balance for me was not there.....I think I'm more disappointed in the fact that it doesn't really work for everybody in the way that it's supposed to work.

(Robert)

Graduated Approach and Person-Centred Planning

The term "graduated approach" refers to a four-stage cycle of assess/plan/do/review. It occurs in education when increasing levels of intensity of support occur in a planned manner (Sewell & Smith, 2021). Class teachers should follow the graduated approach in identifying children who appear to have barriers to accessing the curriculum. At each stage of the cycle (assess/plan/do/review), the educational setting should engage with parents and the child/young person; gaining their insights to inform an effective partnership in assessment and planning of provision. This ensures that the approach highlights and acts upon what is important to a person; thereby, placing the person at the centre of the planning (PCP). It is a process of continual listening and learning; focusing on what is important to someone now and in the future (Hellawell, 2019).

The underlying values of PCP focus on discovering how an individual wants to live their life and what is required to make this possible. This approach applies to all individuals requiring additional support in all situations and across all sectors – education, health and social care. The starting point is the individual, rather than the service provided for them and requires a flexible and responsive approach to address needs, changing circumstances and personal aspirations (Hellawell, 2019). As Robert (parent) described in the previous section on EHCPs, effective PCP relies on equitable knowledge of what is available across all sectors in order to plan provisions that make the individual's life goals possible.

However, the authors argue that effective partnership in co-production and effective person-centred planning is complex. In order for a partnership, based on mutual understanding and trust to be developed, parents must always feel that their role as experts is acknowledged (Cheminais, 2011; Nutbrown et al., 2008; Dyson, 2004) and the challenges of their lived experience recognised. This is difficult because, the relationship between parents and professionals is often polarised: parents striving constantly to get the best for their child and professionals balancing reduced budgets and increased workloads. Effective partnerships can build bridges; allowing honest discussion and negotiation to take place where professionals and parents are treated as equals (Green & Edwards, 2021).

The effectiveness of working in partnership with parents depends, to a large extent, on the views and attitudes of the professionals involved. Partnerships should not be viewed as static; but, as a responsive and collaborative movement towards shared goals based on mutual respect, complementary expertise and a willingness to learn from each other (Swann, 1984, p.293).

Key Strategies to Support Effective Co-production and Partnership Working

Effective co-production involves financial and emotional investment from organisations, professionals, parents and those with SEND.

- Organisations – need to invest in training and ongoing professional development for staff at all levels. Thus ensuring that there is a cohesive and consistent understanding of what is meant by co-production; and, to enable facilitation of co-productive meetings and shared outcomes
- Professionals – need to invest emotionally in co-production; developing trusting relationships and a sense of emotional safety for parents, carers and those with SEND. This will ensure that all participants in the process believe that their contributions are of equal value.
- Parents – need to gain confidence and trust in the system and gain the confidence to participate as experts and equals in meetings.
- People with SEND – need to be given time and opportunity to express their wishes and views whatever form their communication takes.

Conclusion

The concept of co-production reflects an often too gradual change in attitude towards those with SEND. With inclusion, equality and empowerment at its heart, effective co-production forms part of a movement towards true partnership working. Co-production represents a willingness by all to learn from and value each other (Swann, 1984, p.293). While there are many challenges in the development of effective person-centred planning and co-produced solutions, the short-term and long-term benefits cannot be underestimated. Its effectiveness is already being seen in practice through the EHCP process. As participants who believe their voices and views are valued and respected, people with SEND and their families gain the confidence to become agents for their own change. At the same time, the changing role of professionals from that of providers of service delivery and support to being the facilitators of shared solutions ensures that power is more equally distributed, collaboration is more effective (Boyle and Harris, 2009) and true partnerships become a realistic possibility:

> I've experienced co-production..., and I know what it feels like and how much stronger it's made me feel......
>
> (Lianna)

Key Take-Aways

- Ensure that there is a shared understanding of what is meant by co-production.
- Ensure that all participants feel that their contributions are equally valued.
- Ensure that the language used is clear, accessible and jargon-free.
- Ensure that emotionally safe spaces are created for meetings (whether virtual or face-to-face).
- Ensure that enough time is booked for co-productive meetings, allowing time to process and understand information.

Topics for Discussion

1. What are the greatest challenges to effective co-production for professionals and families?
2. Is there a clear understanding of what is meant by co-production within the field of SEND?
3. How can professionals support those from "harder to reach" families to gain the confidence to engage more fully in the co-productive process?
4. Is co-production the best form of inclusive practice?

References

Appleton, P. L., & Minchom, P. E. (1991) Models of parent partnership and child development centres. *Child: Care, Health and Development*, 17, 27–38.

Arnold, L., & Hoskin, J. (2021) Cited in Beaton, M.C., Codina, G.N., and Wharton, J.C. (2021) *Leading on Inclusion: The Role of the SENCO.* Oxon: Routledge.

Boswell, N., & Woods, K. (2021) Facilitators and barriers of co-production of services with children and young people within education, health and care services. *Educational and Child Psychology 38*(2), 41–52.

Boyle, D., & Harris, M. (2009) *The Challenge of Co-production.* London: New Economics Foundation.

Brandsen, T., Verschuere, B., & Steen, T. (eds.). (2018) *Co-production and Co-creation: Engaging Citizens in Public Services.* New York: Routledge.

Cahn, E. (2000). *No more throw-away people: The co-production imperative.* London, Edgar Cahn

Care Act (2014) Available at: https://www.legislation.gov.uk/ukpga/2014/23/contents/enacted

Cheminais, R. (2011). *Family Partnership Working: A Guide for Education Practitioners.* London, Sage.

Children and Families Act (2014) Available at: https://www.legislation.gov.uk/ukpga/2014/6/contents/enacted

Cline, T., & Frederickson, N. (2009) *Special Educational Needs, Inclusion and Diversity.* New York: McGraw-Hill Education.

Dyson, A., Farrell, P., Polat, F., Hutcheson, G. & Gallannaugh, F. (2004) *Inclusion and Pupil Achievement.* London: DfES.

Fern, E. (2014) Grown-ups never understand anything by themselves... *Practice: Social Care in Action*, 26(1), 3–22.

Forrest, C. (2013) Adapting to workplace change. Independent nurse.co.uk, 5 March 2013. Available at: www.independentnurse.co.uk/professionalarticle/adapting-to-workplacechange/63721 (Accessed 20 August 2022)

Green, H., & Edwards, B. (2021) Cited in Beaton, M. C., Codina, G. N., & Wharton, J. C. (2021) *Leading on Inclusion: The Role of the SENCO.* Oxon: Routledge.

Groundwater-Smith, S., & Mockler, N. (2016) From data source to co-researchers? Tracing the shift from 'student voice' to student-teacher partnerships in Educational Action Research. *Educational Action Research*, 24(2), 159–176.

Hall, V. (2017) A tale of two narratives: Student voice—what lies before us? *Oxford Review of Education*, 43(2), 180–193.

Hart, R. A. (1997) *Children's Participation: The Theory and Practice of Involving Young Citizens in Community Development and Environmental Care.* London: Earthscan.

Hellawell, B. (2019) *Understanding and Challenging the SEND Code of Practice.* London: SAGE.

INVOLVE. (2016) *Involving Children and Young People in Research: Top Tips and Essential Key Issues for Researchers*. Eastleigh: Involve.

Kilkelly, U., Kilpatrick, R., & Lundy, L. (2005) *Children's Rights in Northern Ireland*. Belfast: Northern Ireland Commissioner for Children and Young People.

Laming, H. (2003) The Victoria Climbie Inquiry. Available at: http://dera.ioe.ac.uk/id/eprint/6086

Nutbrown, C. and Clough, P. (2009) Citizenship and inclusion in the early years: Understanding and responding to children's perspectives on 'belonging'. *International Journal of Early Years Education*, 17(3), pp. 191–206.

Oliver, M. (1986) Social policy and disability: Some theoretical issues. *Disability, Handicap & Society*, 1(1), pp. 5–17.

Realpe, A., & Wallace, L. M. (2010) *What Is Co-production*. London: The Health Foundation.

Rotter, J.B. (1966) Rotter's internal-external control scale. Psychological Monographs: General and *Applied*. APA PsycTests. https://doi.org/10.1037/t01671-000.

Ryan, S. & Runswick-Cole, K. (2008) Repositioning mothers: Mothers, disabled children and disability studies. *Disability & Society*, 23(3), pp. 199–210.

Sewell, A., & Smith, J. (2021) *Introduction to Special Educational Needs, Disability and Inclusion*. Oxon: SAGE.

Tisdall, E.K.M. (2017) Conceptualising children and young people's participation: Examining vulnerability, social accountability and co-production. *The International Journal of Human Rights*, 21(1), pp. 59–75.

Warnock, M. (1979). Children with special needs: the Warnock Report. *British Medical Journal*, 1(6164), p. 667.

Williams, C., Edlin, J., & Beals, F. (2010) Commentary 6: Spaces and structures: Looking from the outside. In B. Percy-Smith & N. Thomas (eds.) *A Handbook of Children and Young People's Participation: Perspectives from Theory and Practice* (pp. 287–290). London: Routledge.

6 Transitions

> it felt like our child's whole future was in someone else's hands.
>
> (Hannah)

Introduction

Whatever our needs or abilities, our lives are shaped by the transitions we experience and the way in which we respond to them. Whether anticipated or unanticipated, transitions involve emotional adjustment to a new situation. For children with SEND (Special Educational Needs and Disabilities), the emotional and physical adjustments involved with transition affect not just the child but the whole family. For parents, periods of transition are a particular source of stress and anxiety and often become synonymous with a sense of "doing battle" with professionals, authorities and settings:

> my experience, is that they would always assume that what you're asking for is unreasonable and therefore, before you even start negotiating, it is always a fight.
>
> (Ava)

This chapter will explore theories and concepts of transition, the impact it has on children with SEND and their families; highlighting potential strategies to ensure more effective partnership working during these critical times in the life of a child with SEND.

Definitions of Transition

The word "transition" is derived from the Latin verb "transitus", meaning to go, to pass over or to move away. It is linked to the word "transient", meaning "to pass through a place without staying". Transitions should, therefore, be perceived as a journey; a movement from the familiar to the new, a temporary situation between two periods of stability (Levinson, 1986). Parkes (1971) argues that psychosocially transition should be defined as "the abandonment of one set of assumptions and the development of a fresh set", while Anderson et al. (2012, p.49) posit that the period of transition should lead to "positive emergent growth". This ends once acceptance of the new situation creates a sense of renewed stability. Rosenkoetter et al. (2007) explain that transitions should be considered as a process, often extending over months rather than as a single action or point in time. Transitions are often linked to feelings of anxiety and stress, caused by a sense of uncertainty and instability. Schlossberg (1995) defines transitions as events which lead to a change in relationships, routines, assumptions or roles. Whether they are perceived as positive (starting school or college, getting a new wheelchair) or negative (reduction in support, family breakdown), transitions are always disruptive and disquieting. Inevitably, they create change which necessitates adaptation for all those involved (Schlossberg, 1995). Implicit in every transition is the knowledge that it begins with an ending (Chickering & Schlossberg, 2002); that, moving on inevitably means leaving something behind:

> I was very involved in the pre-school .... I knew all the staff individually and worked very closely with his key worker and I think that the contrast when we went to (special school) I felt that quite starkly in terms of.... I think I lost a lot of control... we didn't even take him

DOI: 10.4324/9781003089506-7

to the front gate you know, he was on transport… it was a sort of, you know, goodbye and thank you and a very stark cut off.

(Susan)

The contrasting emotions of loss and anticipation, grief and excitement, endings and beginnings that are created by transitions, cause a dissonance; an internal battle, which can lead to a heightened emotional state. For those who are transitioning, this can sometimes cause challenging behaviours, while those who are supporting them often experience increased anxiety and stress. For families with children with SEND, this is particularly true; as times of transition (or their child's lack of developmental transition) can become synonymous with missed milestones and on-going battles to ensure that the correct resources are in place.

Transition Theory

The transition theory was developed by Schlossberg in 1984. Although not specific to SEND, the key elements of this theory are useful in promoting a greater understanding of how those who are transitioning might be feeling; whatever their needs or background. The theory consists of two key elements:

- the phases of transition
- taking stock

Phases of Transition

Schlossberg (1984) identified three phases of transition: "moving in", "moving through" and "moving out" (Figure 6.1).

Moving In

This is the assessment and planning stage (Barclay, 2017). For those with SEND, this will include person-centred multi-agency meetings, where the focus of the meeting should be the wants, needs and wishes of the person transitioning and their family. For young people under the age of 25, this would usually be part of an Education, Health and Care Plan (EHCP). This stage is frequently perceived as "doing battle" by parents and carers and can often feel confrontational to professionals. Clarity at this stage is crucial, as miscommunication or misunderstanding can undermine the whole process. At times of high anxiety and worry, it is easy for meanings and messages to be misunderstood (Goleman, 1996). This phase of the transition process often includes paperwork, which can feel overwhelming for parents and carers. At times of high emotion, it is easy for meanings and messages to be misunderstood:

when you get the assessments the EHCPs coming through and everything else, it's a new world. We were just given papers it was said, 'okay, okay sign these papers and your son has been diagnosed with ASD … it was a messy process.

(Robert)

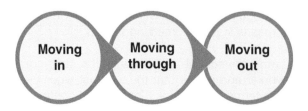

Figure 6.1 Schlossberg's phases of transition (1984).

I was petrified at the paperwork ... because you need you know that you need to hit certain criteria to be able to get the help you need.

(Hannah)

For the person with SEND, the anticipated change can be a cause of high anxiety. For those with an intellectual disability, this phase can be particularly difficult as it will take them time to process and understand the implications of the transition. Clear communication at this stage is essential (including the use of photos, symbols and social stories) as this will limit anxiety caused by uncertainty. The creation of a "safe space", based on a true partnership consisting of trusting relationships, honesty and openness, is key to the effectiveness of the "moving-in" phase of transition for those with SEND and their families.

As one parent stated, what helps is:

good communication, honesty and your ability to ask questions.

(Hannah)

Moving Through

"Moving through" occurs as children, young people and adults physically transition. It is the phase when those transitioning learn about the new situation and what is expected from them (Barclay, 2017). It is the time when new friendships are forged and learning and development takes place. For those with SEND, this phase can take much longer than for those without SEND. Those who are physically impaired will need time to learn to navigate new surroundings and environments; while those who are learning impaired will need time and support to feel included and to process the change. A successful "moving through" phase will, eventually, engender a sense of belonging in those who are transitioning. The importance of "belongingness" was highlighted by Maslow in 1943 and is perceived as an innate human need. For those with a disability or impairment, a sense of belonging is much harder to attain as they "move in" and through the transition process and they need to be supported through the "unconditional positive regard" (Rogers, 1951) of the practitioners and professionals involved.

I wish people could really see (our daughter) for who she is and what she's able to do and recognise the significance of that.

(Jono)

This is supported by Schlossberg who highlighted the concept of "mattering", as underpinning successful transitioning (see later in the chapter).

Moving Out

According to Schlossberg's theory, moving out is the final phase. "Moving out" should represent a smooth transition into the next part of life.

Including a Period of Stability

However, if transition is to be seen as a journey and as the space between two periods of stability (Levinson, 1986), it could be argued that before the "moving out" phase, there is a period of stability. As the transitioner adapts and assimilates, it leads to a period of steady predictability before "moving out" and moving into the next transition. It is only once achievement has occurred in this phase (e.g. a student has graduated, a child has developed some speech and language skills, independent living skills have been learnt) that they advance to the "moving out" phase, which in turn leads into a new "moving in" phase; thus creating a continuous cycle of transition (Figure 6.2).

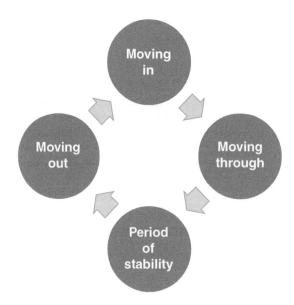

Figure 6.2 Adapted from Schlossberg's transition theory (1984).

Phases of Transition and SEND

For those with a learning impairment, the period of stability is particularly important. A sense of emotional safety is a pre-requisite; in order for learning and individual progress to occur (Van der Kolk, 2014) and this is only possible in times of stability. The sense of impermanence, induced when moving through a transition, means that emotional energy is invested in understanding and processing new information and learning to navigate a new environment with new expectations. It is only when they are in the more stable and settled phase that they can then begin to "move forwards". For those without SEND, "moving through" can involve "moving forwards". But, "moving forward" often does not begin until the first two transition phases are complete and a new period of stability has begun. Therefore, it is recognised that those with SEND may need more time and support to embrace change and to understand new ideas; yet aspirations for those with disabilities have been and remain traditionally low:

> [Some teaching is], so cursory… it's that world of functional skills. It's that, these children, they don't need to learn anything sophisticated or complex because they can't, let's just give them some busy work or let's just fill up their time with…little task.
>
> (Jono)

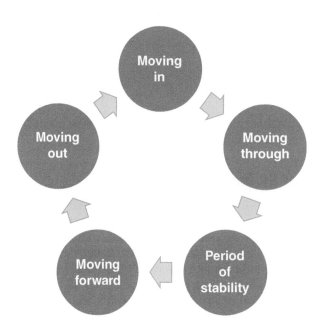

Figure 6.3 SEND transition cycle, adapted from Schlossberg's phases of transition.

If transition is shaped by the idea of movement, as its Latin roots suggest, and if it is defined as passing through a place without staying (see section on definitions), then "moving forwards", cognitively, physically or emotionally, must occur before a transition can be considered to be successful. Therefore, a transition cycle, specific to disability, should include a "moving forward" phase (Figure 6.3).

The concept of "moving forwards" through transitions is reiterated in Chapter 8 of the SEND Code of Practice (2014) where there is a clear expectation that students with SEND will make progress vocationally and/or academically through meaningful work placements and high aspirations. Importantly, there should be no cursory teaching and there should be no repetition of successfully completed learning.

While the SEND transition cycle can be applied to both parents and those who are transitioning, it is important to remember that they might be in different phases of the cycle. For parents, the period of stability is often short-lived as they prepare for the next transition; and while their child is in the "moving forward" and embedding learning phase, the parents are often already moving into the next transition phase. Therefore, person-centred discussions around transition need to be based on an awareness of where individuals are on the transition journey, rather than on a generic agenda. This can be supported by considering the Schlossberg's 4 S's (2008).

Key Elements to Consider at Times of Transition for Those with SEND

Taking Stock (the 4 S's)

Schlossberg (2008) believed that, in order to support successful transitions, it was important to take stock and assess. She believed that four domains needed to be considered (the 4 S's) for the transition (Barclay, 2017):

- Situation – what is currently happening in the life of the person who is transitioning
- Support – what intrinsic and extrinsic support systems do they have
- Self – awareness of who they are and how they are feeling
- Strategies – what way do they have of coping when they are stressed or anxious

Adapting the 4 S's for SEND

This concept of taking stock (2008) is a useful tool for professionals and transitioners at the "moving in" assessment and planning phase of a transition. However, a key element is missing from the 4 S's when considering transitions for those with physical or intellectual impairment. While this framework supports person-centred planning and ensures that the views of the service user are at the centre of any decisions, it does not include taking stock of the views and emotions of the parents, carers and wider family members involved. If true partnerships are to be developed, the 4 S's of all family members need to be considered:

> I don't think we're at the centre, I don't think families are at the centre … they (professionals) always live in this kind of mono-world and they don't always understand the complexity… this is a whole family you're dealing with.
>
> (Tessa)

Therefore, the framework for "taking stock" needs to be adapted to better understand the views and concerns of all members of the family, as well as the person who is transitioning (See Table 6.1). This is supported by Article 8.2 of the SEND Code of Practice (2015), which states that education, health and care services and other agencies should involve parents in discussions about the young person's future. However, it does not mention the wider family.

Table 6.1 SEND – Taking Stock Framework

4 S's	Transitioner	Parent/carer/siblings
Situation	How are you feeling about the transition (describe clearly what will be happening)? Do you know why this is happening now? What are you most worried about when you think about transitioning? Are you worried about anything else that is happening at the moment? What are you looking forward to the most?	How are you feeling about the transition? If this is not what you were hoping for, what will help you feel better about the situation? What are you most worried about? Do you feel that the new setting understands the needs of your son/daughter – brother/sister? If not then what would help them have a better understanding? What do you hope your son/daughter – brother/sister will gain from the new situation? What are you hoping the benefits will be?
Support	Do you know who will be helping you in your new school/job/home? (If staff cannot be present at a transition meeting, use photos)	What resources will help to make the transition successful? What support does your son/daughter – brother/sister need? What support will you need?
Self	What do you think will be difficult for you? What do you think you will be really good at? What do you think you will like the most? How will someone know if you are feeling sad? How will someone know if you are feeling happy? How do you think you will be feeling on your first day?	What will be the hardest part of the transition for you? What would help make it easier? What would help you feel as though you can trust the staff/professionals who will be supporting your son/daughter – brother/sister?
Strategies	Do you know who to talk to if you want to tell someone how you are feeling?	Who will you contact if you feel there is a problem?

Source: Taking stock – adapted from Schlossberg (2008).

Types of Transition

Cairns and Fursland (2007) argue that there are three different types of transition:

1. Universal life transitions – developmental stages and milestones that occur naturally (e.g., walking, talking, puberty, becoming an independent adult).
2. Socially determined transitions – transitions that are expected to occur at times/ages deemed appropriate by society (e.g. going to school, leaving home, starting work).
3. Culturally determined transitions – milestone events or ceremonies that represent a spiritual transition.

Importantly, for families of children and young people with SEND, the first two types of transition can be particularly challenging. The fact that universal and developmental milestones are often delayed or never reached means that, at these times, parents are reminded of what their children may never achieve compared to their peers without SEND:

> as parents, we know what our children might not do in life and that is the fear that drives us every day.
>
> (Robert)

This can trigger depression or chronic sorrow (see chapter 7) and may lead to isolation; as it becomes increasingly difficult to be confronted by their children's peers who able to do things that their children cannot yet and may never be able to do. This is exacerbated at times of socially determined transition. For families of children with SEND, listening to other parents celebrating the achievements of their children as they transition into the next stage of their lives, can often accentuate their sense of exclusion and of "otherness" (Spivak, 1985):

> with mates, I don't know, when similar aged kids were teenagers … and … would get A Levels and go off to University and whatever, I remember thinking then that G won't be doing that. And I remember thinking, 'how am I going to address this,' because I remember feeling angry.
>
> (Dan)

Societal transitions depend on cultural and traditional values and accepted social structures and norms. For those who are not able to follow the traditional life course, who are not always able to meet societal expectations, times of transition can create a sense of alienation and ostracism which has long-term effects including lowered expectations, low self-esteem and low self-worth. Such negative emotional impact could be lessened or ameliorated if societal views on transition were embedded in an Inclusive philosophy. Stereotypically, transitions are viewed as discreet events, representing accepted stages in the life course: school, moving out of home, job, marriage/long-term partner, becoming parents. Those who cannot follow this course frequently feel marginalised and often perceive themselves as failures. If, instead, transitions were perceived as part of a cumulative and individualised journey, with a clear recognition that key times of change are different for everyone but of equal meaning and impact for all: then this negative impact would be lessened.

> I remember saying…, 'well actually, if James got a job in Sainsburys … then I would be absolutely over the moon.' So I kind of made them realise that actually it is not just about him going to University, that (getting a job in Sainsbury) would actually be a fantastic achievement and I would be really happy about that.
>
> (Dan)

Timing

For those with SEND, it is particularly important to ensure that the transition process begins early enough to ensure that they have a clear understanding of what is happening. It is commonly recognised that those who are intellectually impaired take longer to process and understand information than their unimpaired peers, while those with a physical impairment need time to familiarise themselves with a new environment. Therefore, it is important to consider the timing of transition processes in order to allow for clarity and for the views of individuals, families and professionals to be heard. This is emphasised in the Children and Families Act (2014) where professionals are encouraged to support transitions from the moment of diagnosis and schools must introduce the concept of transition into adulthood at year nine when children are 14.

Mattering and Belonging

Recognised as a time of stress, disruption and uncertainty transitions can lead to a loss of sense of purpose (Frankl, 1984) and of familiar anchor points (van der Kolk, 2014), resulting in feelings of marginalisation and insignificance (Schlossberg, 1985). In her study of transitioning, Schlossberg became convinced of the importance of "mattering" in the transition process. Mattering is the perception of being important to others, of believing that someone is interested in and concerned about us (Marshall, 2001; Rosenberg & McCullough, 1981), which, in turn, creates the sense of belonging that is so important for health and happiness (Wilcock, 1998). Importantly, this is true for parents wanting to make sure that their views matter to the professionals they are working with. Mattering emerges from the development of trusting relationships and true partnerships and plays an integral role in successful transitions:

Care is not about charity and it's not about… some kind of faith or belief, it's just about that recognition and acknowledgement of other people, as other people.

(Jono)

Knowing that someone cares is linked to a positive sense of self and enhanced self-esteem. For those with impairments, who often feel excluded or forgotten, identification of adults or peers who will care about and be interested in them, will lead to a sense of emotional safety which could be the difference between a positive or a negative transition experience. This is particularly true for parents. Mattering is relational and for parents, struggling with isolation, feeling disempowered and exhausted by the transition process, knowing that there is someone who cares can make the difference between giving up and carrying on:

the person I did find extremely helpful was actually from Home Start…she said, 'repeat the facts until you get what you want. Be factual, non emotional and back up why you're saying what you're saying,' and actually that massively, massively helped me. And she was just really kind. She called herself Nanny McPhee. She would just to be there when I needed… her…She was amazing.

(Hannah)

Perceptions of Transition in SEND

Parents

A Time of Stress and Worry

For parents of children and young people with SEND, transitions represent a permanent source of stress, worry and concern:

I am nervous about the future… it's a massive thing moving to the college but then it's the next step that's more worrying… beyond the college because I know that there seems to be.. a cliff edge.

(Hannah)

This concept of transition, as a time of anxiety and uncertainty, supports Anderson's view, (2012) that any definition of transition must include not only change but also an individual's perception of change. Every transition represents something different to each person involved (e.g. a child with SEND may be looking forward to starting a new school and perceive it as something positive and exciting; a parent might perceive the transition as a fight to get the right support for their child, whereas professionals might perceive the change as problematic, involving paperwork, long meetings and battles over budgeting restrictions). This mixture of opposing responses to the process of transition may result in feelings of anger, resentment and frustration, thereby leading to a breakdown in the relationship between parents, schools and the professionals involved.

Letting Go

The fact that every transition begins with an ending (Bridges & Mitchell, 2000) means that letting go (emotionally and sometimes physically) can be viewed as a precursor to effective transitioning. For parents of children with SEND, intensely aware of the vulnerability of their son or daughter, this can be particularly difficult. They worry that they have made the wrong decision and that their son or daughter will not be able to cope without them (Codd & Hewitt, 2021; Richardson, 1989). Therefore, times of transition become synonymous with a sense of guilt and a lack of control:

you've got to be tough and you got to get used to letting go, and if you don't, you know it will just eat you up and it will destroy you in the end …. So I think I'm doing the right thing, … although it is heart breaking,

(Robert)

Agency

Bandura (1977) first recognised the power of self-efficacy, the belief that we are more successful if we feel that we have some control over what happens to us. During transitions, parents and those with impairments often feel a loss of agency believing that decisions are made by the system, rather than by those with SEND and their families (Richardson, 1989):

> I think there's still a lot of professionals making decisions for people … I think it's still working like that.. we're now heading towards adult services. It's like, you have no… you..just give up everything you've ever worked to get because you're going to lose all decision-making power
>
> (Tina)

Transitions are more successful and have better outcomes when everyone is involved in the decision-making process (Kelly, 2013; Kraemer et al., 2003). This is supported through current legislation (The Children and Families Act, 2014 and the Care Act, 2014) which emphasises the importance of person-centred, co-productive planning at all stages of a child's, young person's and adult's life. However, it is important for professionals to recognise that many families lack the confidence to participate fully in transition and planning meetings. Those from lower socio-economic backgrounds or minorities might lack the confidence or self-belief to fully engage in discussions (Kelly, 2013). Importantly, they are more likely to have an external locus of control (Rotter, 1966) believing that they have little control over what happens to them rather than a strong internal locus of control, sometimes linked to higher levels of cultural and social capital (Bourdieu, 1966) where they believe that their words and actions influence what happens to them:

> I don't know if it's just that we're brave enough but it is not just middle-class parents, you get all sorts of parents who are also very articulate and able to make their case and have the time to do it. But there are a lot of people that don't have those skills or the time to do it and who don't have the time or energy whatever, or don't have the courage… yeah courage maybe too.
>
> (Tina)

Person-centred planning is recognised as an embedded and accepted part of the transition process, it is hoped that all parents, carers and participants will gain the confidence to honestly represent their views.

The Impact of Non-event, Transitions that Do Not Happen

Within the transition framework, understanding of the impact of "non-events" is particularly important for both children, young adults, parents and professionals. A non-event is a transition that is expected but does not occur (Evans et al., 1998). This can add a sense of deflation and disappointment to the emotional dissonance already being experienced:

> we moved house … and we wrote to the Educational Department… to say we were moving into the area and that our daughter had a statement of special educational needs and was due to attend a speech and language unit and we had chosen to move (there), because there was a primary school with a speech and language unit in it, which would also be fine for her siblings to attend … the local authority said, '… absolutely no way. We would have to reassess her and…go through the whole process again.'
>
> (Nigel)

The realisation that an anticipated transition, developmental or physical, is not going to happen (e.g. a child does not learn to speak, the offered supported living place does not materialise, speech therapy will not be funded) often leaves parents of children with SEND feeling let down by the system and distrustful of professionals. Experience of transitional non-events occurs more often in families of children and young people with SEND than in other families. This is often as a consequence of requests for placements, settings or resources which will have a significant financial implication for local authorities or health trusts and on which they cannot agree. As with all areas of collaborative and partnership working, the impact on non-transitions can be mitigated against through honest and trusting relationships with professionals and clear communication.

Professionals

Emotional Impact

Importantly, consideration needs to be given of the emotional impact of transitions on the professionals involved, whether from education, health or social care. While families of children with SEND often feel supported by professionals, times of transition can cause polarisation. This can result in parents perceiving professionals as a barrier to accessing the support that would best meet the needs of their child:

> I think there is an assumption that if you are asking for something, whether it's more support at the school you're currently at or a different placement, that, that must be unreasonable... people have an allocation of money and it's all about that.
>
> (Ava)

Conflict and Dissonance

Times of transition can become periods of conflict. This can be particularly difficult for professionals; who are often the conduit for other organisations they represent. A study by Fisher and Byrne (2012) found that although professionals, working with students with intellectual disabilities believed that much of their person-centred work enhanced the well-being of their service users, they sometimes felt implicit organisational pressure to pursue practices which contradicted this. This left them feeling uneasy, representing a view or action that they did not believe to be correct nor that fitted with their internal philosophy. The emotional labour (Hochschild, 1983) involved in these situations and the idea that professionals must conjure up appropriate feelings to make those they are working with feel better and subdue inappropriate ones – the belief that what they are doing is not in the best interests of the client (Newman et al., 2009) is defined by Hochschild (1983) as the commodification of emotions and is a cause of stress and anxiety for those who experience it. Times of transition often represent periods of intense emotional labour for professionals who are not only dealing with the repercussions of such internal dissonance, but frequently absorb the anxiety and often anger of the families and individuals they are supporting.

Conclusion

While the aim of any transition is "positive emergent growth" (Anderson et al., 2012), positive adaptation is a process which takes emotional time and effort on the part of those transitioning as well as those supporting the transition. This is particularly the case for children, young people and adults with SEND. For those with learning impairment, cognitively processing and understanding changing expectations and support can be challenging and exhausting, while for those with physical disabilities, becoming familiar with a new environment and ensuring consistent accessibility can take time and patience from all involved in the transition process. For parents and carers, transition can be a reminder of missed milestones and become synonymous with "doing battle". While professionals supporting transitions can feel that they are in a constant state of defensive dissonance; unique to transitions is the concept that they are simultaneously a beginning and an ending, while Levinson's (1986) definition of transition as the time between two periods of stability represents a sense of disruption and unsettledness. Planning for transitions early is highlighted in the Children and Families Act (2014) however legislation is not the key to effective transitions. Instead, there is a need for parents, carers and professionals to work together in order that support is given to those with impairments on their transition journey.

Key Takeaways

- Parents and carers and those with SEND might be at different phases of the same transition journey, needing different support and understanding.
- Parents often perceive transitions as a cyclical battle. Times of transition can become synonymous with missed milestones for parents and carers; this can trigger chronic sorrow or depression'.
- Transitions are more likely to be positive, if parents, families and service users are included in the decision-making process.
- Non-events, transitions that do not happen, can cause as much stress and have as much emotional impact as transitions that do happen.
- Families often perceive transitions as battles rather than a process.

Topics for Discussion

1. Why are transitions through the life course so difficult for everyone and especially difficult for those with SEND?
2. Why are non-events, transitions that do not occur, particularly difficult for individuals with SEND?
3. What can professionals put in place to ensure that transitions become easier for those with SEND and their families?
4. How can effective partnership working ensure that transitions occur more smoothly?

References

Anderson, M. L., Goodman, J., & Schlossberg, N. K. (2012) *Counseling Adults in Transition: Linking Schlossberg's Theory with Practice in a Diverse World* (4th ed.) New York: Springer Publishing Company.

Bandura, A. (1977) Self-efficacy: Toward a unifying theory of behavioral change. *Psychological Review*, 84(2), 191.

Barclay, S. R. (2017) Schlossberg's transition theory. In W. Killam & S. Degges-White (eds.) *College Student Development: Applying Theory to Practice on the Diverse Campus*. New York, NY: Springer Publishing Company, pp. 23–34.

Barsade, S. G. (2002) The ripple effect: Emotional contagion and its influence on group behavior. *Administrative Science Quarterly*, 47(4), 644–675.

Bourdieu, P. (1966) Condition de classe et position de classe. *Archives européennes de Sociologie*, VII(2), 201–223.

Bridges, W., & Mitchell, S. (2000) Leading transition: A new model for change. *Leader to Leader*, 16(3), 30–36.

Cairns, K., & Fursland, E. (2008) *Transitions and Endings: A Training Programme*. London: British Association for Adoption & Fostering 2008.

Care Act (2014) Available at: https://www.legislation.gov.uk/ukpga/2014/23/contents/enacted

Chickering, A. W., & Schlossberg, N. K. (2002) *Getting the Most Out of College*. New York: Pearson College Division.

Children and Families Act (2014) Available at: https://www.legislation.gov.uk/ukpga/2014/6/contents/enacted

Codd, J., & Hewitt, O. (2021) Having a son or daughter with an intellectual disability transition to adulthood: A parental perspective. *British Journal of Learning Disabilities*, 49(1), 39–51.

Erin, E. A. (2020) *Disability as Diversity: Developing Cultural Competence*. Oxford: Oxford University Press (Academy of Rehabilitation Psychology Series). Available at: https://search.ebscohost.com/login.aspx?direct=true&db=nlebk&AN=2275141&site=eds-live (Accessed 12 August 2022).

Evans, F., & Guido-Di, B. (1998) *Student Development in College: Theory, Research, and Practice*. San Francisco, CA: Jossey Bass.

Fisher, P., & Byrne, V. (2012) Identity, emotion and the internal goods of practice: a study of learning disability professionals. *Sociology of Health Illness*, 34(1), 79–94. ISSN 1467–9566 https://doi.org/10.11 11/j.1467-9566.2011.01365 (Accessed 12 August 2022)

Frankl, V. E. (1984) *Man's Search for Meaning: An Introduction to Logotherapy*. New York: Simon & Schuster.

Goleman, D. (1996) *Emotional Intelligence: Why It Can Matter More Than IQ*. London. Bloomsbury Publishing.

Goodman, J., Schlossberg, N. K., & Anderson, M. L. (2006) *Counseling Adults in Transition: Linking Practice with Theory*. New York: Springer Publishing Co.

Hochschild, A. R. (1983) *The Managed Heart: Commercialization of Human Feeling*. Berkeley: University of California Press.

Kelly, B. (2013) *'Don't Box Me In': Disability, Identity and Transitions to Young Adult Life*. Belfast: Queen's University Belfast.

Kraemer, B. R., McIntyre, L. L., & Blacher, J. (2003) Quality of life for young adults with mental retardation during transition. *Mental Retardation*, 41(4), 250–262.

Levinson, D. J. (1986) A conception of adult development. *American Psychologist*, 41(1), 3–13.

Marshall, S. K. (2001) Do I matter? Construct validation of adolescents' perceived mattering to parents and friends. *Journal of Adolescence*, 24(4), 473–490.

Newman, M. A., Guy, M. E., & Mastracci, S. H. (2009) Beyond cognition: Affective leadership and emotional labor. *Public Administration Review*, 69(1), 6–20. https://doi.org/10.1111/j.1540–6210.2008.01935.x.

Parkes, C. M. (1971) Psycho-social transitions: A field for study. *Social Science & Medicine*, 5(2), 101–115.

Richardson, A. (1989) Letting go: A mother's view. *Disability, Handicap and Society*, 4(1), 81–92. https://doi.org/10.1080/02674648966780061.

Richardson, M., West, M. A., Day, P., & Stuart, S. (1989) Children with developmental disabilities in the child welfare system: A national survey. *Child Welfare*, 68(6), 605–613.

Rogers, C. (1951) *Client-Centered Therapy*. Cambridge, MA: The Riverside Press.

Rosenkoetter, S.E., Hains, A.H., & Dogaru, C. (2007) Successful transitions for young children with disabilities and their families: Roles of school social workers. *Children & Schools*, 29(1), 25–34.

Rosenberg, M., & McCullough, B. C. (1981) Mattering: Inferred significance and mental health among adolescents. *Research in Community and Mental Health*, 2, 163–182.

Rotter, J. (1966) Generalized expectancies for internal versus external control of reinforcement. *Psychological Monographs*, 80(1), 609.

Schlossberg, N. K. (1984) Exploring the adult years. In A. M. Rogers & C. J. Scheirer (eds.), *The G. Stanley Hall lecture Series* (Vol. 4). Washington: American Psychological Association, pp. 105–154. https://psycnet.apa.org/doi/10.1037/10089-003

Schlossberg, N. Waters, E., & Goodman, J. (1995) *Adults in Transition, Linking Practice with Theory* (2nd ed.). New York: Springer Publishing.

Schlossberg, N. (2008) *Overwhelmed: Coping with Life's Ups and Downs* (2nd ed.). Lanham, MD: Evans.

Spivak, G. C. (1985) The Rani of Sirmur: An essay in reading the archives. *History and Theory*, 24(3), 247–272.

van der Kolk, B. A. (2014) *The Body Keeps the Score: Brain, Mind, and Body in the Healing of Trauma*. London: Penguin.

Wilcock, A. A. (1998) Reflections on doing, being and becoming. *Canadian Journal of Occupational Therapy*, 65, 248–256.

7 Chronic Sorrow

This does not stop. … It doesn't stop and we get older sadly.

(Lianna)

Introduction

The concept of chronic sorrow has been understood for many years and is increasingly being recognised as playing a crucial role in shaping professional responses to families with children with SEND (special educational needs and disability). However, discussion of chronic sorrow is rarely included in training programmes for either health, education or social care professionals. A professional understanding of chronic sorrow, what it is, how it is experienced by parents of children with SEND and the wider family, is essential if true partnerships are to be developed. This chapter explores definitions of chronic sorrow, its cumulative impact on families and how professionals can recognise potential triggers. It offers strategies to ensure that understanding of the concept can be used as a catalyst for developing positive relationships between families and professionals and as a way in which those relationships can be strengthened and embedded.

History of Chronic Sorrow

Chronic sorrow was first conceptualised by sociologist and counsellor, Simon Olshansky, in 1982 while he was working with parents of children with SEND. As he listened to their stories, he became aware of the difference between the grief induced by their growing understanding of the life-changing impact of their child's impairment and the grief experienced by those who were bereaved. Olshansky identified the emotions felt by parents as:

"the normal pervasive psychological response in the suffering of parents dealing with mentally disabled children."

(Olshansky, 1982)

More recently, chronic sorrow has been identified by health professionals as impacting on those who have a family member with a chronic illness (Coughlin & Sethares, 2017). It is hoped that improving knowledge and understanding of chronic sorrow will lead to the prioritising of compassionate care in all professions, based on honesty, kindness and respect (Coughlin & Sethares, 2017).

Understanding Chronic Sorrow

Chronic sorrow is a periodically recurring, progressive form of grief with no predictable end (Burke et al., 1992; Eakes et al., 1998). It begins at birth or with a diagnosis of impairment and continues throughout the life course of the child or parent. It is experienced cyclically as the result of trigger events which cause families to re-live the grief they experience at the initial diagnosis. Unlike the sadness felt when someone dies, the sorrow experienced by the parents of children with SEND is not time-limited nor finite (Olshansky, 1982; Roos, 2017). Instead, it is an ambiguous (Boss, 1999) and living loss (Roos, 2017) which re-occurs each time parents are reminded of what their children have not achieved or as the result of missed milestones:

DOI: 10.4324/9781003089506-8

> I guess its birthdays..., you think 'oh.. he's 10 or 11 but still not talking.' ... it's like grief, it just kind of sneaks up on you.
>
> (Susan)

Or when their children are unable to experience the expected rites of passage that are societal markers of growth and development:

> I remember with mates .... when similar aged kids were teenagers ... and their kids would get "A" Levels and go off to university ..., I remember thinking then that James won't be doing that. ...
>
> (Dan)

The importance and impact of Olshansky's, subsequently Roos', work remains critical for professionals as they try to build positive relationships and true partnerships with the parents and individuals with SEND. In particular, Olshansky's explanation that the grief experienced by parents is a "normal" reaction began to change perceptions and understanding of the parental response to their situation. Based on his observations and work with parents, Olshansky understood that the "grief", experienced by parents of children with SEND was not pathological but was a natural human response to a confusing, often frightening situation and an altered and uncertain future. Nor is it a neurotic response from "controlling and overprotective parents" as had historically been believed (Roos, 2017) but "a normal reaction to an abnormal situation" (Wikler et al., 1981).

Double-Grief

Unique to chronic sorrow is the fact that when parents discover their child has an impairment, they experience a form of double grief:

- Grief for the loss of their "dreamed of child" (Roos, 2017)
- Grief for the future their child will now never have (Olshansky, 1982)

The duality of this parallel grief creates a depth of sorrow that can often intensify as the child grows and the awareness of the loss of the "normal" life that neither they nor their child will now experience, deepens. This loss, in particular, incubates and re-emerges with every missed milestone or rite of passage, where the discrepancy between the lived experience and the hoped for future is repeatedly re-enforced (Roos, 2017). With each re-experiencing of the loss, hope is depleted:

> I can see maybe what her life could be and all the things she's not going to be able to do
>
> (Tessa)

The Difference between Chronic Sorrow and Traditional Grief

Grief as the result of bereavement is painful, personal and all-consuming. This is also true of chronic sorrow but what differentiates it from the traditional understanding of grief is that it is not time-limited; and due to its cyclical nature, it cannot be contained within the accepted stages of grief (Kubler Ross, 1969). As a living loss, it can be experienced in varying degrees throughout the life course of the child or parent (Bryant & Peck, 2009) but with a continuing depth of emotion often comparable to that of the original grief (Wikler et al., 1981). Melvin (2004) argue that chronic sorrow is not caused by a single event but that it is the consequence of repeated loss triggered by different events:

> it almost gets worse as they get older........
>
> (Tessa)

This sense of loss accompanies parents throughout their lives, preventing families from experiencing the peace that comes with acceptance. They are left instead with a sense of unresolved, unboundaried loss that Boss (2006) calls ambiguous loss. This ambiguity magnifies the sense of confusion and long-term uncertainty that often surrounds the lives of children with SEND and their families. Lack of closure, lack of definitive endings to the emotions being experienced, a pervasive sense of lingering sadness (Olshansky, 1982) that cannot always be explained (Hawke, 1996) and the cyclical re-emergence of grief are all part of the ambiguity. This lack of closure can act as a barrier to progress, causing uncertainty and confusion and parents and children to become stuck, unable to move forward (Hawley & DeHaan, 1996):

The progressive sorrow and the experiencing of dual grief leads to the (sometimes gradual) loss of hope and optimism specific to becoming a parent: the hope that children will grow up healthy and happy (Ott & Ladd, 2010). This is a hope that is always present at birth and continues as children develop and grow, often intensifying as developmental and social milestones are met and celebrated. Sometimes, with an initial diagnosis, this hope becomes a longing

> I suppose early on you might have thought that she would have been more able than she's going to be... I suppose as time goes by, you adjust to all sorts of things
>
> (Ava)

Interwoven with chronic sorrow, is a sense of this hope diminishing as the child grows and the unknown future becomes a familiar, often complicated and exhausting, present.

> It's not going to stop is it? It's just going to go on and on and I'm 63 and I'm really tired.
>
> (Robert)

Experiencing and Re-experiencing Chronic Sorrow

The cyclical nature of chronic sorrow means that there are periods of time when its impact is lesser and parents feel happy and are able to adapt positively to their situation (Busch, 2015). This tends to be at times when their child has fewer medical issues, when caring duties are lower or when unmet milestones and worries about the future are not casting a shadow over the present.

> I think there's moments where you just despair, but equally there's some moments that you can really cherish. I mean the silly little things, like he made us coffee the other day, and it is just like those little things you know.
>
> (Hope)

Although parents experience happiness, the circumstances which create the initial sorrow have not changed and the attainment of a sense of stasis, calmness and balance is usually temporary. At some point, it is likely that the sorrow will be re-triggered and re-experienced with the same or a cumulatively greater degree of intensity (Olshansky, 1982; Wikler et al., 1981; Bryant & Peck, 2009; Roos, 2017).

Triggers

> all it takes is a trigger... and we go into fight or flight mode and it's because we don't know what to do.
>
> (Lianna)

Chronic sorrow is triggered by events that are both expected and unexpected. As their children grow, parents begin to recognise times or activities that might be potential triggers: social events where the difference between their child and others is accentuated, celebrations of rites of passage that their children will never achieve, parents' evenings and sports days. Many of these triggers are the result of socially constructed expectations where parents find themselves making excuses for their child's delay:

> The fact that, he had no language…often people would say 'oh you know, no language, it comes when its ready and maybe it is because he is a second child and you have a very articulate first child, ….' But I think as a Mum you know,
>
> (Susan)

In Fischer's (1994) study of chronic sorrow, a mother explains that the sorrow rising inside her in these situations made an honest explanation too upsetting; these feelings can also emerge as the result of an unexpected action or event:

> you tick along and then things happen that kind of expose her phenomenal vulnerability. Like…., the thing recently…she's managed to spend over £2000 on rubbish on the Internet …., it does highlight her lack of safety within society.
>
> (Ava)

Melvin and Heater (2004) describe each of these reactions to unpredictable events as "mini-losses", while Eakes et al. (1998) explain that triggering events are just one part of a cycle of chronic sorrow which also includes the periods of happiness, periods of concern when parents seek assistance, episodes of sorrow and degrees of recovery. But the re-experiencing of the sorrow adds to its cumulative impact which can eventually lead to depression or high levels of anxiety (Roos, 2017).

A driving factor in the re-experiencing of chronic sorrow is the love the parents feel for their child, the need to protect them and the growing awareness of their vulnerability as they grow older. Often children with SEND and their parents or primary carers experience an emotional inter-dependence which can exacerbate the cycle of chronic sorrow.

> she (our daughter,) asked me how old I was and if I was going to die soon. Then told me she was going to die when I die.
>
> (Tessa)

While parents often worry that acknowledging their sorrow could be perceived as a lack of love, it is, in fact, a reflection of the intensity of their emotion and a natural consequence of their love for and desire to protect their child. Parents often experience cognitive dissonance where they try to justify these two competing emotions:

> If I experience sorrow, I cannot love my child enough
> versus
> I cannot love my child enough without experiencing sorrow

While neither of these statements are necessarily true, they reflect the continual internal conflict felt by parents.

Triggers of Chronic Sorrow

There is sometimes a mismatch between what parents know to be triggers and what profession-als perceive as potential triggers. While diagnosis, missed developmental milestones, puberty, a younger sibling overtaking an older sibling and transition to adult services were recognised by both as potential triggers, professionals tend to overestimate the emotional impact of early experiences and underestimate those of later experiences including 21st birthdays (Wikler et al., 1981). Working together to recognise triggers will help professionals to gain a greater under-standing of individual needs and help parents to develop more effective coping strategies and accept the legitimacy of their sorrow.

> the first time I heard chronic sorrow I thought, I know what that is. I felt it. And I suppose it's a recognition and it's … a relief that it's okay to feel sad.
>
> (Hope)

Emotional States Linked to Chronic Sorrow

While the emotional upheaval linked to chronic sorrow is individualised and uniquely experienced, research into episodic and permanent emotional responses has led to a greater understanding of its impact on parents and families (Olshansky, 1982; Eakes, 1995; Hawke, 1996; Ott & Ladd, 2010; Roos, 2002, 2017). Building on the work of Olshansky (1982) Roos (2002, 2017) identified 15 potential states of emotions that families might experience including shock, disbelief, physical symptoms, such as headaches and fatigue, guilt, heightened levels of anxiety, social isolation, societal rejection and emotional upheaval. Added to these is a sense of self-loss (Goffman, 1963), and intermittent despair linked to a constant and often overwhelming fear for a future where they are not there to care for and protect their child.

Initial Emotional State: Shock/Confusion/Disorientation and Denial

Initial diagnosis can leave parents in a state of shock, flooded with unexpected emotions and with a loss of the normal anchor points that support the transition into parenthood. This overwhelming limbic reaction creates a flight-fight-freeze response (Goleman, 1995) in the brain making it difficult to process information or to understand what is happening. The consequent sense of disconnection and confusion leaves parents feeling lost and vulnerable and unaware of the dual grief they are beginning to experience.

> I was in limbo. … Numb…. Dismayed…. ….. I was getting all these urban myths about feeding, …, not quite knowing what to do or what to say….. it disables you….. No one tells you that Down syndrome babies don't really cry. No one told me that and I just thought I had a really brilliant baby.
>
> (Laura)

The chronic nature of parental sorrow means that this shock response is often not an isolated occurrence. The state of permanent vulnerability and health precarity that accompanies disability mean that parents often have to experience unexpected or traumatic news throughout the life course of their child, creating a renewed sense of disorientation and confusion

Amidst this emotional turmoil and sense of intangible loss, there is often a denial of the situation in which parents find themselves. Acceptance can take time, complicated by the loss of the idealised child and the anticipated future, parents often experience an ostrich phase (Ulrich & Bauer, 1984) where they bury their heads in the sand or cling on to hope.

> you do have those strange cases where children can have brain damage then somehow are absolutely fine… and you're desperately hoping that this might be you. You might be the one in a million.
>
> (Tracy)

> we could not accept the idea that our son was going to be difficult. The way he thinks, the way he lives …. We always believe … in my culture … that if it's a disease it's curable (or) … it's just a passing phase …
>
> (Robert)

In order to avoid facing the reality of their child's diagnosis or to stem the feelings of loss and sadness, parents will often initially choose to "opt out" of support groups or of accepting help that is being offered.

> I didn't want to see children with Down syndrome, I didn't want to see them anywhere, I didn't want to go to any of the sessions that were held at the centres and stuff like that I just didn't want to see it….. I wasn't ready to look at it.
>
> (Lianna)

Emergent Emotional State: Self-loss and Guilt

Feelings of sadness and grief that emerge with acknowledgement are not just for the child but for the parents themselves. Hawke (1996) explains how he can never remember a time when he did not feel sad as the father of a child with SEND, but his sadness was often for himself, rather than his son. Often this sense of loss of the imagined – self is intertwined with feelings of guilt (how can I feel sad when my child is suffering? Has this happened because of something I did *"could it have been avoided if I'd been more careful" (*Tessa)) and anger (why has this happened to us? *I do despair sometimes, you know, I'm just thinking, "what have I done? Why do I deserve this?"*(Robert)) It's all my fault (*"I felt really guilty that it had all come out of my body so I do… somehow think it was my fault".* (Tessa)) Belief that they can never be a good-enough parent to their child with an impairment and that they had ruined the life of the siblings (*"It felt like I had ruined Sam's life, I hadn't given him the sibling he had wanted… I just felt… that I absolutely let him down and it's just continued".* (Tracy))

These feelings of guilt can lead to a sense of worthlessness and shame, highlighting the loss of self as an idealised parent and constructing a re-shaped self-view as a failure, a belief that is re-enforced each time their child's disability is brought back into focus or awareness of their "difference" is highlighted. For fathers, in particular, the sense of failure is linked to a sense of inadequacy that they have not been able to provide a healthy or better life for their child (Uribe-Morales et al., 2022).

> I just feel that I should have provided a better house that was big enough, you know…. I just feel it's all a big failure.
>
> (Mike)

Ongoing Emotional State: Emotional Labour, Heightened Anxiety, Exhaustion, Fear for the Future

Parents of children who have a disability, take on a lifelong, often physically and emotionally exhausting, caring role. The care may involve managing challenging or aggressive behaviours or it might be physical, including lifting, handling and personal care. Physical symptoms can be chronic – constantly present, or cumulative – becoming worse over time e.g. back problems from lifting, or periodic and cyclical, triggered by events or unexpected health problems for their child. Implicit in this caring role is Hochschild's concept of unpaid emotional work (1963) where parents constantly suppress genuine emotions of worry and fear in order to portray more positive or appropriate emotions (Ashforth & Humprhey, 1993) to comfort, soothe and protect their child. The discrepancy between their genuine emotions and the emotions they portray to their children causes an unresolved internal conflict. The combined cumulative effort involved in unremitting caring responsibilities and the cognitive dissonance caused by emotional labour and ongoing sorrow can lead to long-term physical damage and emotional exhaustion.

As with all issues related to chronic sorrow, the physical and emotional labour are not time-limited and the knowledge that their children will need lifelong support becomes a constant concern for parents of children with SEND. "What will happen in the future" is consistently highlighted as one of their greatest fears (Northington, 2000; Bettle & Latimer, 2009).

> one of the worst things of having a disabled child, is thinking about time and the future what happens when we are not around and that's something that haunts me, terrifies me…. I'm terrified at Chloe just being left to die…
>
> (Jono)

> What's going to happen? What happens if we're not here?
>
> (Hope)

> the ultimate worry is when we're not about, who's going to look after him,
>
> (Lianna)

The distress caused by this fear for the future often remains unresolved and demands high levels of effort from parents in order to protect their child with SEND and siblings from sensing their anxiety. Inseparable from the fear for the future is the sense of guilt that siblings will eventually carry the burden of responsibility, mixed with a sense of panic that they might not.

> I don't want to put the responsibility on my daughter because we didn't have her for this. But I'm aware that you know, she's part of the family and she wants to be close to him.
>
> (Laura)

> I can look at my daughter who is 12 and I can go she's got plenty she wanted to do…, but I mean she said it once, she said, 'well you know one day James will have to live with me,
>
> (Lianna)

Isolation: Societal and Emotional

Underpinning the sorrow and guilt experienced by parents is a constant and increasing sense of isolation, both societal and emotional. Often this begins with a perceived lack of societal understanding of their situation, demanding continual and exhausting explanations leading to a sense of otherness (Spivak, 1985) and eventual rejection.

> I have stopped even explaining ……sometimes…, I just pretend like I'm not there…. We explain a lot to society… we take care of society but they don't take care of us
>
> (Robert)

As with many elements of chronic sorrow, rejection and the resultant social and emotional isolation is experienced on two levels, first through the rejection of their child

> The social isolation of your child… having to witness that,…is really difficult,
>
> (Jono)

and then their own rejection:

> we lost friends, … we lost close family and we lost visitors to the house.
>
> (Robert)

Parents can begin to feel that they are living in a parallel universe, cut off from the rest of the world (Roos, 2017).

> I remember, one sports day when (he) ran in the opposite direction to everyone else, just thinking this is the journey that you go on with a child with special needs, you always feel like you're running in a different direction.
>
> (Susan)

Understanding Chronic Sorrow for Professionals

Understanding the concept and impact of chronic sorrow can help professionals to build trusting and empathetic relationships with families. Key to the creation of a successful partnership is the understanding that many parents never resolve their complex emotional response to the situation they find themselves in (Wikler et al., 1981) and professionals should not expect them to do so. Instead, they should help them to identify triggers to chronic sorrow and support them to lessen the impact. Professionals should be:

1. Compassionate – show understanding of the intensity of the re-occurring sadness
2. Helpful – help parents to identify potential triggers to chronic sorrow
3. Resourceful – work out the best way to support the family and prevent triggers

4. Open-minded – be aware that triggers are not always predictable
5. Non-judgemental – remember that the sorrow is not pathological but a normal response
6. Impactful – ensure interactions are meaningful and result in agreed actions
7. Caring – take time to listen, empathise and support. Challenge feelings of guilt

Gender Differences

While these emotional states will be experienced by both parents, Coughlin and Sethares (2017) found in their integrated literature review that generally mothers reported more intense and permanent experiences of chronic sorrow than fathers who are more able to resolve their grief but, according to Hobdell and Deatrick (1996), are more worried about social stigma than mothers. It is argued that since mothers are, traditionally, more often the primary carer, they have a greater awareness of the limitations caused by the disability and of the impact this has on life chances for their child and their family.

Why Knowing about Chronic Sorrow Matters

Understanding the theory of chronic sorrow can help both parents and professionals. Many parents are unaware of the concept and often feel guilty at the sadness they feel. Knowing that their response is normal, that they are not alone is often a relief which can mitigate the feelings of loneliness and guilt.

> I think before I knew about it (chronic sorrow)…it was a lot, lot worse.
>
> (Hope)

Knowledge of chronic sorrow can help professionals to better understand and empathise with parents. Consideration of its cumulative, cyclical nature (Roos, 2017) and familiarity with potential triggers can help both in developing an empathetic understanding of the lived experience and in supporting parents to better understand the cause of their grief.

Conclusion

While chronic sorrow is known to be experienced by almost all parents of children with SEND, the profound impact it has on their lives has often been unrecognised or minimised by professionals. As a continually re-experienced living loss, chronic sorrow forms an integral part of the complex parental response to a continually challenging situation. Professionals need to acknowledge its ubiquity and recognise that its existence prevents parents from reaching a stage of complete acceptance. Professionals and parents therefore need to work together to recognise trigger points and to accept that periods of sadness are inevitable. The long-term consequences of chronic sorrow, including isolation, depression, anxiety, emotional exhaustion and a sense of otherness, need to be recognised and supportive strategies put in place. Olshansky (1967) believed that a wise practitioner should use understanding of chronic sorrow as a basis for intervention.
It is time for practitioners to be wise.

Key Take-Aways

1. Parents experience a dual loss at birth or diagnosis: the loss of the wished-for child and the loss of the dreamed-of future
2. Chronic sorrow is a normal response to an abnormal situation

3. Triggers can be expected or unexpected
4. Chronic sorrow is a cyclical, living loss
5. Professionals should not expect parents to reach a stage of acceptance

Topics for Discussion

1. How might knowledge of chronic sorrow inform practice and encourage the development of stronger partnerships?
2. What could help parents to deal with the impact of chronic sorrow?
3. Are there similarities as well as differences between the traditional concept of grief and chronic sorrow?
4. Would it help parents if the concept of chronic sorrow was explained to them when they receive the original diagnosis of SEND?

References

Ashforth, B. E., & Humphrey, R. H. (1995) Emotion in the workplace: A reappraisal. *Human Relations*, 48(2), 97–125.

Bettle, A. M., & Latimer, M. A. (2009) Maternal coping and adaptation: A case study examination of chronic sorrow in caring for an adolescent with a progressive neurodegenerative disease. *Canadian Journal of Neuroscience Nursing*, 31(4), 15–21.

Boss, P. (1999) *Ambiguous Loss: Learning to Live with Unresolved Grief*. Cambridge, MA: Harvard University Press.

Boss, P. (2006) *Loss, Trauma, and Resilience: Therapeutic Work with Ambiguous Loss*. New York: W. W. Norton & Co.

Busch, S. (2015) *Chronic Sorrow in Parenting a Child with a Disability*. Available at: https://susanellisonbusch.com/chronic-sorrow-in-parenting-a-child-with-a-disability/

Bryant, D., Peck, L., & American Library Association (2010) Encyclopedia of death and the human experience. *Reference & User Services Quarterly*, 49(3), 289–290.

Burke, M., Hainsworth, A., Eakes, G., & Lindgren, L. (1992) Current knowledge and research on chronic sorrow: A foundation for inquiry. *Death Studies*, 16(3), 231–245.

Coughlin, M., & Sethares, K. (2017) Chronic sorrow in parents of children with a chronic illness or disability: An integrative literature. *Journal of Pediatric Nursing*, 37, 108–116.

Eakes, G. G. (1995) Chronic sorrow: The lived experience of parents of chronically mentally ill individuals. *Archives of Psychiatric Nursing*, IX, 77–84.

Eakes, G., Burke, M. H., & Hainsworth, M. A. (1998) Middle-range theory of chronic sorrow. *Journal of Nursing Scholarship*, 30, 179–184.

Eakes, G., Burke, M., & Hainsworth, M. (1999) Chronic sorrow: The experiences of bereaved individuals. *Illness, Crisis & Loss*, 7, 172–182.

Peterson, S., & Bredow, T. (eds.) (2009) Middle Range Theories: Application to Nursing Research. Lippincott Williams & Wilkins.

Fischer, S. (1994) Fathers are caregivers too! *The Exceptional Parent*, 2, 43–44. Available at: http://www.eparent.com

Goffman, W. (1963) *Stigma: Notes on the Management of a Spoiled Identity*. Englewood Cliffs, NJ: Prentice-Hall.

Goleman, D. (1995) *Emotional Intelligence*. Bantam Books, Inc. London: Bloomsbury.

Hawke, W. (1996) The lone father. *The Exceptional Parent*, 26, 28. Available at: http://www.eparent.com.

Hawley, D. R., & DeHaan, L. (1996) Toward a definition of family resilience: Integrating life span and family perspectives. *Family Process*, 35, 284–298. Available at: http://www.familyprocess.org

Hobdell, E. F., & Deatrick, J. A. (1996) Chronic sorrow: A content analysis of parental differences. *Journal of Genetic Counseling*, 5(2), 57–68.

Jennings, J. (1987) Elderly parents as caregivers for their dependent children. *Social Work*, 32, 430–433.

Kubler-Ross, E. (1969) *On Death and Dying*. New York: MacMillan.

Lichtenstein, B., Laska, M. K., & Clair, J. M. (2002) Chronic sorrow in the HIV positive patient: Issues of race, gender, and social support. *AIDS Patient Care and STDs*, 16(1), 27–37. https://doi.org/10.1089/108729102753429370

Melvin, C. S. (2004) Suffering and chronic sorrow: Characteristics and a paradigm for nursing interventions. *International Journal for Human Caring*, 8(2), 41–47.

Northington, L. (2000) Chronic sorrow in caregivers of school age children with sickle cell disease: A grounded theory approach. *Issues in Comprehensive Pediatric Nursing*, 23(3), 141–154.

Olshansky, S. (1982) Chronic sorrow: A response to having a mentally defective child. *Social Casework*, 43, 190–193. Available at: http://www.familiesinsociety.org/default.asp

Ott, P., & Ladd, D. (2010) The blending of Boss's concept of ambiguous loss and Olshansky's concept of chronic sorrow: A case study of a family with a child who has significant disabilities ambiguous loss and chronic sorrow. *Journal of Creativity in Mental Health*, 5, 74–86.

Roos, S. (2002) *Chronic Sorrow: A Living Loss*. New York: Brunner-Routledge.

Roos, S. (2017) *Chronic Sorrow: A Living Loss* (2nd ed.). London, Taylor and Francis.

Seari, S., Jr. (1978) Stages of parent reaction: Mainstreaming. Except. *Parent* (April), 23–27.

Sobel, S., & Cowan, C. B. (2003) Ambiguous loss and disenfranchised grief: The impact of DNA predictive testing on the family as a system. *Family Process*, 42, 47–57. https://doi.org/10.1111/j.1545–5300.2003.00047

Spivak, G. C. (1985) The Rani of Sirmur: An essay in reading the archives. *History and Theory*, 24(3), 247–272.

Ulrich, M. E., & Bauer, A. M. (2003). Levels of awareness: A closer look at communication between parents and professionals. *Teaching Exceptional Children*, 35(6), 20–23.

Uribe-Morales, B., Cantero-Garlito, P., & Cipriano-Crespo, C. (2022) Fathers in the care of children with disabilities: An exploratory qualitative study. *Healthcare*, 10(1), 14. Available at: https://doi.org/10.3390/healthcare10010014.

Wikler, L., Wasow, M., & Hatfield, E. (1981) Chronic sorrow revisited: Parent vs. professional depiction of the adjustment of parents of mentally retarded children. *American Journal of Orthopsychiatry*, 51(1), 63.

Wikler, L. (1983) Chronic stresses of families of mentally retarded children. In L. Wikler & M. Keenan (eds.) *Developmental Disabilities: No Longer a Private Tragedy*. Silver Spring, MD: National Association of Social Workers and Washington, DC: American Association on Mental Deficiency, pp. 102–110.

8 Resilience

Magic Bullet; Buzz Word, or Something Else?

Chris Smethurst

Introduction

Resilience – It is an elegant word, tripping easily from the tongue and filling the pages of policy documents, self-help books and academic journals. Resilience is aspirational, motivating and reassuring (Gill & Orgad, 2018). In a world where "keep calm and carry on" has become a ubiquitous and inoffensive motif on cups, posters and tea towels: resilience has apparently entered seamlessly into public consciousness. However, this chapter will examine in more detail the potentially problematic aspects of our contemporary understanding of resilience. Crucially, it will explore whether resilience is an adequate term to capture the experience of parents of children with disabilities as they navigate the challenges they face.

In my work at the university and elsewhere, I often ask people to consider what the word "resilience" means to them. In the following pages, we will explore some of the academic and professional definitions of the term. These usually have some resonance with individuals' own experience, but often fall short. Words and phrases associated with resilience include: "grit", "determination", "perseverance"; "bouncing back"; "coping" and "positive adaptation to adversity" (Fletcher & Sarkar, 2013). However, these words seem to me to be overly focused on behaviours, actions and skills. They fail to capture what resilience *feels* like, if in fact, it feels like anything distinctive at all. Arguably, even a focus on the individual experience of resilience runs the risk of being overly focused on the psychological: resilience is so much more than what goes on inside our heads, our thoughts, feelings and personality traits. As we shall see in this chapter, resilience is also about connectedness with others; the formal, but sometimes ad hoc, web of practical, social and emotional interdependence that characterises our lives.

Grotberg (1997) explores resilience from a human rights perspective. Her work focuses on children, yet her conclusions are arguably equally relevant to adults. Critically, in order to thrive, children have a right to expect: trusting relationships; to be *supported* to be autonomous and independent; access to adequate health, welfare and educational services; to be encouraged to communicate, which involves being heard. Grotberg also examines personality traits, behaviours and attitudes; but, crucially, without the right support, these are not likely to be enough to sustain resilience, certainly over an extended period (Seccombe, 2002; Hickman, 2018).

In essence, Grotberg's work encourages us not to think of resilience as merely something that is focused on an individual's or family's skills or attributes, but on the wider social, economic and political dimensions. Nevertheless, there is arguably something of the courageous about the word "resilience"; Estêvão et al. (2017) explore the growing dominance of the heroic narrative of resilience in public policy: one where individuals discover previously hidden and untapped reserves of resourcefulness and courage. However, people rarely define themselves in heroic terms and, as this chapter will explore, a focus on individuals "triumphing against the odds" is deeply problematic. The testimonies of the parents in this book reveal a great deal of "keeping calm and carrying on"; a lot of perseverance in the face of bureaucratic obstruction and delay; a consistent experience of battling and frustration. The overriding message is that the parents do this because they have to; and that in a different world they would not need to. Therefore, there is a risk in reframing these very real struggles as psychological hurdles that can be overcome merely by a change of mindset and some practical exercises.

I write from a position where I do not know what resilience "feels like" for parents of children with disabilities. I am an outsider looking in. Therefore, in writing this chapter, I do not wish to patronise, state the obvious or indeed fall into the trap of focusing on individuals and families, disaggregated from a wider social, economic and political context. In short, if this context was more favourable, perhaps resilience would be less essential. Consequently, the elements of this chapter that focus on building resilience have been drawn from work conducted with parents, which they have reported to be useful. Specifically, parents have

DOI: 10.4324/9781003089506-9

stated that, in gaining a deeper understanding of the mind and body's reactions to stress and fatigue, this has been helpful in identifying those factors which underpin or undermine their own resilience. From my own experience of working in the field of resilience, I have learnt that there are many useful skills and techniques that can be practised and mastered. However, understanding what we are experiencing and why goes a long way in demystifying resilience. Similarly, this knowledge is helpful in depathologising the natural human responses to uncertainty, change and adversity.

Following a brief overview of the evolution of resilience as a concept, we will explore strengths and limitations of relevant research conducted with parents of children with disabilities and explore two key themes: fatigue and stress.

As If by Magic, Resilience Appeared?

The concept of resilience has its historical roots in the physical sciences and engineering (Taşan-Kok et al., 2013). The ability of materials and structures to withstand shocks and stresses has an obvious resonance with the manner in which human beings absorb and respond to physical and psychological challenges. Consequently, from the 1950s onwards, resilience emerged as a term increasingly applied to themes as varied as Holocaust survival (Frankl, 1959); burnout (Maslach & Jackson, 1981; Maslach et al., 1997); child poverty (Garmezy, 1993); loss and bereavement (Coifman et al., 2007); abuse and trauma (Van der Kolk, 2014).

More recently, Rufat (2015) argues that resilience has become a portmanteau word, one to which different meanings and definitions can be attached according to context. Its very plasticity has contributed to its popularity and its surprising and rapid evolution to occupy a key space in political, business and public consciousness. In addition to its being a malleable and flexible term, the association of resilience with positivity contributes to its appeal. The framing of resilience as "ordinary magic" (Masten, 2015) captures this ambiguity and positivity: resilience is special, but also commonplace?

Masten (2015, p.4) stresses that resilience "arises from ordinary resources and processes", she is keen to emphasise that resilience is not the province of exceptional people and that most people are resilient most of the time. However, Rufat (2015) contends that resilience is a term which is at risk of losing its value: in short, if resilience is a concept where "everyone can rediscover their own meaning" (Rufat, 2015, p.201), what exactly does resilience *mean*?

Southwick et al. (2014) suggest that resilience is often viewed as being one or all of the following: as a trait, a process or an outcome. However, Fletcher and Sarkar (2013) note that most definitions of resilience share a unifying feature: positive adaptation to adversity. Southwick also states that resilience is often viewed as being present or absent. This is a false binary that does not reflect individuals' lived experience. For example, resilience may best be seen as a continuum or spectrum; which may change over time, or according to circumstances or environment (Pietrzak & Southwick, 2011). This seems particularly important when one considers that human beings' perception of their own ability to cope will vary over time and according to context.

Returning to the themes of resilience as a portmanteau word and its association with positivity, it may be helpful to revisit the work of Alaszewski (1998) in relation to what is arguably another portmanteau word: "risk". Alaszewski conceptualises the word "risk" as being the visible tip of an iceberg. Beneath the surface of the neutral-sounding term, there lies hidden a range of other meanings; including, anxiety, fear, blame and harm. Arguably, resilience can be conceptualised in a similar way: beneath the surface may lurk anxiety; the fear of not being resilient; of not being good enough; the fear of failure and the awareness of the potential negative consequences of things beyond one's control. These themes are reflected in the interviews with parents:

> I don't even know how to help my son. And that was one of the things that I would... you know, you lie awake at night just thinking, you know what, would I call myself a good dad?
>
> (Dan)

> I just feel that I should have provided…. I just feel that I should have provided a better house that was big enough, you know…. I just feel it's all a big failure and I'm going to have to give him up eventually…
>
> (Nigel)

One of the central problems with some contemporary views of resilience is that it can be seen as essentially an *individualised* approach to adversity, with distinctly moral overtones. "Resilience is not a static trait that some have and others lack" (Lown et al., 2015, p.708); yet, it remains associated with character, specifically grit, self-reliance and resourcefulness. As such, it aligns with neoliberal conceptualisations of the ideal citizen who, when facing adversity, looks first to their own resources and those of their families and places few expectations and demands on the state (Bull & Allen, 2018; Burman, 2018; Walker & Cooper, 2011). Thus, individuals are ultimately responsible for their own emotional wellbeing and material welfare; crises are personal ones, divorced from their wider political and economic context (Bottrell, 2013).

Whether it is through heroic endeavour (Estêvão et al., 2017) or cheerful perseverance (Patterson et al, 2009), a non-critical embrace of the tenets of resilience subtly affirms that; stress, anxiety and material and psychological insecurity are the natural human condition, and it is for the individual, not the state, nor indeed wider society, to ameliorate their effects (Evans & Reid, 2015). From here, it is not too great a step for resilience to be weaponised, for individuals and families to be blamed for being not resilient, or not resilient enough (Walsh, 2003; Bottrell, 2013; Vasquez, 2022). Some authors have noted that the rise of resilience in policy discourse has existed in parallel with cuts to public services and real-term erosion of household income levels (Bottrell, 2013; Fenton, 2020; McRobbie, 2020). Failure to navigate these, often catastrophic, consequences for individual and family wellbeing are, at least for the working class, reframed as psychological deficits; the product of fecklessness, psychological dependency and lifestyle choice (Smethurst, 2017).

Resilience is not something that is solely required by the working class, as they navigate the insecurities of modern life. Gill and Orgad (2018) explore the intersection between class, gender and resilience. In particular, they note the societal injunctions placed upon middle-class women to be, "The Amazing Bounce-Backable Woman". Both in popular culture and in political discourse, women are presented as resourceful, adaptable and resilient; often in positive contrast to men. Women are invited to reframe life's challenges as opportunities to banish self-doubt and engage with the possibilities for psychological self-improvement. Within this context, adversity can be presented as emancipatory; an opportunity for women to discover their hidden reservoirs of resourcefulness. In addition, Gill and Orgad (2018) note that media stories often present the misfortunes experienced by women as "a blessing in disguise"; for example, the restricted life chances of women who have been forced to give up a career to care for their children only to discover that it was the best thing they have ever done.

It could be suggested that narratives of middle-class resilience, regardless of gender, reflect the essentially meritocratic worldview of British political discourse: that the capacity to "get on" in society is primarily a product of personal ability and self-discipline (Littler, 2013; Evans & Tilley, 2016). Fundamental to this worldview is an assumption that individuals possess the means to control their own destinies. This seems somewhat at odds with the testimonies of many of the parents interviewed for this book; who are somewhat hostage to the vagaries of social policy and the seemingly capricious decision-making of officialdom:

> I think that you know for so many years, the support and the guidance that's available to parents, carers and the disabled, so much of it is hidden, or it is buried within these technocratic bureaucratic systems and kind of deliberately if I'm honest. Only those who've got that kind of tenacity and an educational level are able to access it
>
> (Susan)

> I think we had a lot of battles and we battled and battled again, and they thought we were wrong and we just stuck to our guns.
>
> (Jules)

In summary, it is problematic to view resilience uncritically; certainly divorced from its economic and social context. Resilience training, skills and techniques alone can be viewed as something of a "sticking plaster"; first aid interventions for the consequences of a wider social political and economic malaise (Seccombe, 2002; Hickman, 2018). With this in mind, it is useful to explore the literature that focuses specifically on parents of children with disabilities.

Parents of Children with Disabilities: "Beating the Odds"?

Heiman (2002) interviewed 32 parents of children with a disability and reported similar irritations and struggles to those parents interviewed for this book. A belief in the child, a realistic understanding and acceptance of the disability coupled with an optimistic outlook were characteristics associated with resilience. However, in this and other studies, it is clear that resilience was not something that could be achieved on one's own: competent professional interventions, material and social support are also identified as critical (Heiman, 2002). These conclusions parallel those of Hart et al. (2014) who explored the evidence base for resilience-building strategies for disabled children and young people. Nevertheless, they conclude that most resilience literature uncritically adopts a medical or psychological perspective on disability: there is limited consideration of how the intersection of disability, exclusion, disadvantage and adversity impacts upon resilience. Critically, there is little evidence of the active inclusion of disabled children and young people in the design and evaluation of effective resilience-building projects.

Hart et al. (2014) suggest that a frustrating aspect of much of the literature is that it focuses on relatively small-scale amelioration of the status quo. In short, although there is recognition of the impact of structural discrimination and disadvantage, the onus largely remains upon the individual or family to develop the resources and strategies to cope with the world the way it is. Seccombe (2002) provides a helpful encapsulation of these problems: many approaches to strengthening resilience at an individual level can merely be seen as a means of beating the odds. Instead, a focus on addressing systemic disadvantage may have the benefit of "changing the odds".

Knight (2014) identifies a similar problematic trend within the research with families with a child with an intellectual disability. She notes that a particular focus has been on the adaptive strategies of mothers, what she identifies as the "theme of the good mother". She argues that the relative neglect of the socio-political foundations of resilience risks further marginalisation of families. Similarly, a number of studies highlight parental awareness of the judgemental attitudes of both professionals and the wider public to both parents and their disabled children (Wade et al., 2007; Osborne & Reed, 2008; Ryan & Quinlan, 2018). These are likely to compound feelings of guilt and inadequacy, of not being "good enough", which appear to be particularly prevalent amongst parents of children with disabilities (Hornby, 1992; Nixon & Singer, 2002; Findler et al., 2016). This is not a product of some shared psychological characteristics of parents of disabled children, but rather a consequence of the need to compensate for a society that is not constructed to provide adequate support, and is both judgemental and stigmatising (Courtney et al., 2018). It is therefore unsurprising that parents may find that this ongoing struggle may be exhausting, isolating and lead them to question their own abilities as parents (Findler et al., 2016).

The Way We Live Now? The Impact on Resilience

There has been considerable research interest in the manner in which the sheer demands of modern life can wear people down; emotionally, physically and cognitively. For example, the American sociologist Arlie Hochschild writes of Western societies being consumed by a cult of "busyness"; where individuals internalise an expectation to be continually active, can feel guilty if they are not and find it difficult to stop. Busyness is, to an extent, a product of the societal expectation on individuals to resolve the conflicting demands of both family and work (Hochschild, 2007, 2013). Clouston (2015) draws on the work of Wilcock (1999) and Hammell (2004) to identify the key elements of a psychologically meaningful and balanced life. They suggest that our lives consist of four key elements: "doing", "being", "belonging" and "becoming". "Doing" is straightforward to understand; it consists of things like work, caring tasks study, domestic tasks and so on. "Being" is the time when we stop and allow ourselves time to think or to do nothing much at all, to recharge our batteries; "belonging" is the time we spend with family, friends and devote to our relationships with others. "Becoming" equates to feeling that we are developing as an individual over time. "Becoming" gives us a sense of achievement and is important to self-esteem, self-confidence and life satisfaction. All four elements were necessary for us to lead relatively contented lives; but, that the pressures of the modern world frequently result in us not paying enough time and attention to some of them. Parents interviewed for this book are clear about the pressures of not having enough time. The following quote is illustrative:

> When you're dealing with a disabled child with high needs, then you have very little capacity and time to manage that
>
> (Tessa)

Parents are very familiar with the experience of not having enough hours in the day to achieve what they need to. When exploring this, some parents have found the concepts of "doing", "being", "belonging" and "becoming" to be useful in understanding those elements of their lives which get prioritised and those which get sacrificed. An exercise which illustrates the proportion of the waking day that is spent on each of Wilcock's four elements requires us to consider the hours taken up on an average day by creating a simple bar chart (Table 8.1).

When I have conducted this exercise, most people, whether they are parents or not, spend the majority of their waking hours "doing". However, for parents of children with disabilities, this pattern is particularly pronounced; often with little or no time devoted to "being" or "becoming". Some parents report that "belonging" is similarly compromised with little time available for meaningful relationships outside the immediate family unit. Even within the immediate family, parents are often concerned that there is at least a risk of neglecting relationships. What is evident is that parents typically have little time for themselves, and what time they do have often has to be negotiated or planned in intricate detail. The following quote illustrates some of the challenges faced:

> They spend all their time looking after this child, but because I want to make my own way and I want to have a life as well I guess that's what makes it really hard
>
> (Matthew)

Writing 20 years ago, Everingham (2002) explored the breakdown of the temporal boundaries between work and family life and the disproportionate impact on women with caring responsibilities. As a mother, she experienced time through a sense of loss, an absence of free time and the necessity of negotiating and organising time, not just for herself, but for other family members.

Table 8.1 Doing, Being, Becoming, Belonging – Self-assessment Tool

	Doing	Being	Becoming	Belonging
12 hours				
11 hours				
10 hours				
9 hours				
8 hours				
7 hours				
6 hours				
5 hours				
4 hours				
3 hours				
2 hours				
1 hours				
0 hours				

These experiences, shared by many if not all parents, are perhaps more acute for parents of disabled children. For example, the additional demands of coordinating and delivering the practical aspects of care require complex strategic planning on a daily basis (Courtney et al., 2018). This is both time consuming and cognitively and emotionally demanding. In addition, parents are often experiencing continual anxiety about the fragility of intricate care arrangements; not least, the vulnerability of any outside support to being either reduced or withdrawn:

> It's all going to be a mess again this is how it is you know if you depend on (state support). You just never... you should always try and steer clear of state benefits because they'll just look after you until you become competent and then they'll stab you in the back, so that's why it's very foolish to depend.
>
> (Evelyn)

A key feature of contemporary Western societies is the tacit acceptance that the demands of work require prioritisation over all other aspects of our lives (Hochschild, 2012). The notion of work-life balance (WLB) is central to these debates. However, the concept of WLB is, in itself, problematic; the literature reflecting a range of different definitions (Lewis & Beauregard, 2018). Perhaps, this is unsurprising, given the essentially subjective and individual perception of what constitutes WLB and its impact on wellbeing (Gröpel & Kuhl, 2009; Hasan et al., 2020). This is somewhat complicated, because for the individual, work creates both negative demands and positive psychological and material benefits, and these vary between individuals.

In addition, the introduction of new communication technologies, including both email and smart phones, has created increasingly fluid boundaries between work and home life (Allen et al., 2021). Although some workers welcome this additional "flexibility", for carers this is not always matched by correspondingly supportive and flexible employer working practices (Manoudi et al., 2018; Matheson et al., 2020; Yeandle, 2020). Hochschild (1997) states that, for many employers, the ideal worker has "zero-drag"; they are continually available to work whatever hours are required unencumbered by any competing commitments or responsibilities. Some parents interviewed for this book have found this balancing act impossible to manage:

> But the other thing that does, that no one understands is the ruinous effect on your economic life. No one, no one can comprehend.... everyone says, well you're just a failure, you know, that's why you ended up like you have. Have you ever tried to look after, you know and hold down the job? You cannot hold a job, therefore you can't buy a house, everything, your whole life is ruined. And because you can't hold down, it's like 'why? Why? Why?' well who's going to look after him 13 weeks of the year?
>
> (Lianna)

> I've gone back to work full time and now I have realised that I'm too old to work full time and I just think, 'oh well I just can't bloody win now. The one time I can go back to work, I've gone back to work and it's too hard and I can't do it, I'm just exhausted all time.'
>
> (Nigel)

Sleep, Fatigue and Resilience

Fatigue, sleep loss and exhaustion were consistent themes arising from the interviews undertaken for this book. The experience of sleep deprivation and chronic fatigue is reflected in the literature concerning parents of children with disabilities: here, it is correlated with decision fatigue, compassion fatigue, stress, anxiety and depression (Seymour et al., 2013; Micsinszki et al., 2018; Davenport & Zolnikov, 2021). High levels of fatigue are also reported in children with physical disabilities, to a level comparable with children with cancer (Maher et al., 2015). More recently, studies have explored the impact of sleep loss and fatigue upon psychological resilience (Hughes et al., 2018; Mantua et al., 2021). Similarly, children with autism experience high levels of fatigue in comparison to other children (Keville et al., 2021). Fatigue in children with physical disabilities correlates with physical inactivity, poverty and discomfort during sleep; children with autism typically display neurological features that create shallow and disturbed sleep patterns (Cortesi et al., 2010; Mazurek & Petroski, 2015).

The recommended daily dose of sleep, across the lifespan, is as follows:

Babies 4–12 months old	12–16 hours (includes naps)
Toddlers 1–2 years old	11–14 hours (includes naps)
Children 3–5 years old	10–13 hours (includes naps)
Children 6–12 years old	9–12 hours
Teenagers 13–18 years old	8–10 hours
Adult (19–60s)	7–9 hours
Older adult	7–8 hours

(Watson et al., 2015; Mireku, 2021).

Although the number of hours of sleep is critical, the quality of sleep is equally important (Walker, 2017). For children with physical disabilities and for children with autism, disturbed or poor-quality sleep may have a number of emotional and behavioural impacts; including irritability, anxiety and depression (Cortesi et al., 2010; Mazurek & Petroski, 2015). These effects replicate the consequences of sleep deprivation for adults which include: disrupted blood sugar levels, rigidity in thinking and cognitive fixation; difficulty adapting to abnormal or changing situations; difficulties in reasoning and decision-making; depression; anxiety; mood swings and irritation (Walker, 2017). It is not too broad a stretch of the imagination to suggest that sleep-deprived adults, caring for sleep-deprived children, could create a potentially problematic mix of emotions and behaviours. These, in turn, would be likely to exacerbate the challenges of being a parent. Successful parenting is heavily reliant on the on higher executive functioning of the brain (Kienhuis et al., 2010). This will come as no surprise to parents who may experience the continual necessity of attempting to anticipate their child's needs and behaviour while making a myriad of complex decisions. On the latter point, Sollisch (2016) estimates that adults in Western societies make 35,000 decisions a day. This can lead to decision fatigue, where the individual may exhibit impulsivity, passivity, avoidance, diminished executive function and less physiological endurance (Pignatiello et al., 2020). Furthermore, people with decision fatigue "experience things more intensely … frustrations seem more irritating than usual" (Tierney, 2011, p.33).

The impact of sleep disturbance on our emotions and cognitive performance can be insidious; in effect, people get used to being tired (Walker, 2017). However, the impact of sleep loss on cognitive performance is quite stark: after four hours of sleep for six nights, an adult's cognitive performance is the same as going without sleep for 24 hours; after six nights of four hours' sleep, their performance is the same as being awake for 48 hours; ten days of six hours' sleep is equivalent of being awake for 24 hours (Van Dongen et al., 2003; Walker, 2017). Therefore, it is unsurprising that fatigue correlates with parents' feelings of lack of competence (Giallo et al., 2013; Dunning et al., 2013). More recent research has indicated that fatigue negatively impacts on the human ability to feel compassion (Angelhoff et al., 2018; Ben Simon et al., 2022); and, that parents who are sleep-deprived may feel more emotionally detached. Evidently, this is something that could compound feelings of inadequacy and could create anxiety.

In summary, sleep loss inhibits cognitive performance; diminishes humans' ability to regulate their emotions and increases feelings of emotional detachment and anxiety. However, it is often the case that individuals may not appreciate the causal relationship between sleep loss, their emotions and cognitive ability (Walker, 2017):

> I haven't slept for so long at this point and obviously I didn't realise at the time that (it was impacting mental health)
>
> (Hope)

> You doubt yourself, you doubt your validity. You doubt your own mental health, which makes it worse. You know, you haven't slept for a few years.
>
> (Jules)

Stress and Resilience

Fatigue contributes to enhanced levels of perceived stress in parents (Dunning et al., 2013). In the popular imagination, stress is often seen as indivisible from doing too much in too little time, whether too much be work, caring responsibilities or the juggling of both. Parents of children with disabilities certainly face high demands and are frequently time poor. However, a third element of the stress equation is the contribution of a sense of control or lack of it. As a psychological trait, feeling that one has agency and control over our lives mitigates against stress and is a key predictor of resilience (Kinman & Grant, 2010). Nevertheless, a sense of control is not determined solely by personality and mindset. Individuals can cope with high demands if they have actual control over them and are not facing challenges without support (Theorell, 2020). However, the parents interviewed for this book frequently report feelings of powerlessness and bureaucratic systems that seem designed to disempower them:

> You felt like your whole child future was in someone else's hands
>
> (Nigel)

> Sometimes my voice was not heard. Sometimes I felt "bullied". Bullied to accept they were right and I was wrong. I felt intimidated – if I was challenging them, or asking them for explanation. I got told by the head of primary ASD in a special school that I was wasting staff time, I had to chase staff at school for a response. Again, I felt that I was the black sheep. This caused me stress and had an impact on my confidence.
>
> (Lori)

A consistent theme of the interviews was the parents' experience of feeling they were in a constant battle.

> There's very much an opinion that if you were asking for something, which is not the thing that… what you must be asking for as a parent must be unreasonable. That is the assumption that is made all the way along the line.
>
> (Tessa)

> Before you even start negotiating, it is always a fight. They expect your requests to be unreasonable and too expensive
>
> (Nigel)

> And we battled and battled again, and they thought we were wrong and we just stuck to our guns
>
> (Lori)

This constant battling is, in itself, stressful. However, parents report the stress of *anticipating* conflict; particular sources of stress being meetings with health, education and social care authorities. The brain is structured to anticipate threat in order to keep us safe (Van der Kolk, 2014). The human stress response suffers from two key features that are likely to exacerbate the stresses of modern life. Firstly, the structures and processes that keep us safe developed relatively early in human evolutionary history. As such, they lack the sophistication necessary to provide a nuanced appraisal and response to stressful events. Secondly, the brain operates on what may be described as a "safety first" principle. Consequently, in response to *potentially* harmful events, the brain triggers physiological and psychological responses which tend to be over-reactions to the actual threat (Van der Kolk, 2014). These can involve anticipatory anxiety, where people experience stress reactions to what *might* happen (Salceanu & Luminita, 2020), or a situation where the stress response receives repeated low-level triggers and does not switch off (Clouston, 2015).

Although humans are generally aware of what stress *feels* like, the impacts upon mental performance and resilience are perhaps less well known. When the potential for threat exists, glucose gets pumped into the blood stream to prepare the body for action. When the glucose reaches the brain, it stimulates the release of hormones called glucocorticoids. These impact upon our conscious brain by impairing memory and slowing our cognitive processes. We may experience this as forgetfulness, "brain fog" and difficulties stringing a sentence together; in short, we may feel mentally overwhelmed. Conversely, glucocorticoids work on the unconscious brain, where feelings and emotional memories are stored, and have the effect of amplifying those associated with stress and anxiety. Because these are unconscious, we may not be able to consciously pinpoint exactly what is worrying us; the brain simply retrieves emotional memories of similar bad things that happened to us in the past. The brain is not sufficiently evolved to fine tune its response to an objective appraisal of the situation. Its purpose is to make us pay attention to something that may be unpleasant or harmful and, by making it seem really bad, prompt us into taking action or avoidance. The consequences for resilience are that our ability to feel in control may be impaired. As with fatigue, our ability to think straight, make decisions and gain an objective sense of proportion about a problem may be compromised. In addition, we may experience unpleasant physical and psychological symptoms which undermine our ability to cope.

Many of the psychological interventions, reviewed in the literature on parental resilience, deal with the management of the symptoms of the human stress response. These approaches directly reflect the burgeoning interest in, and appetite for, skills-based methodologies for developing resilience. Although these have value and have proven effectiveness, they arguably do little to address the underlying economic, political and social causes for the symptoms they suppress. This may be as frustrating for the professionals working with parents as for the parents themselves. Therefore, it seems appropriate to end this chapter with a summary of "what works" for parents as described by parents themselves.

Conclusion

Supporting Resilience: What Works?

Advice for Professionals

- Parents need to feel valued and respected.
- Parents want to be more involved in their child's journey (learning and development).
- Professionals are valued who have respect for and confidence in parents' skills.
- Parents need information and assistance navigating bureaucracy, systems and the boundaries between organisational and professional roles.

It can be seen that these points closely correlate with the features of Grotberg's human rights approach to resilience: trusting relationships; to be *supported* to be autonomous and independent; access to adequate health, welfare and educational services; to be encouraged to communicate, which involves being heard (Grotberg, 1997). In addition, it is evident that these features of resilience mitigate against the feelings of powerlessness and loss of control which are key stressors (Theorell, 2020).

These final words encapsulate the value of mutual support, but also the hopes for fellow parents:

> When I see other parents start on the journey, and you just wish like, okay you know, I wish I could walk with you but I know this is going to be your walk. I wish I could be there for you when you need support. So, this is the idea of the wish that I have: but with that wish as well is to hope that they have people to speak to, they have facilities in place when they need them, and with that is the (hope) that they will have the best advice and information that they want when they need it
>
> (Hannah)

Key Take-Aways: Advice from Parents to Parents

- Establishing and maintaining routines gives structure and enhances feelings of control and efficacy.
- *You learn.... patience. Which is interesting because it's not something that you should learn but it is something that we get in abundance sometimes. But we also learn to accept things,*

in a way we cannot change. But also, we have a different view of what hope is,..., I think it's the celebration of the short-term successes that we have. ...... So there's little things where we will celebrate the little things in our lives (Lori)

- *(Remembering that) it's just finding another route for you to get there and you will get there and it might take a lot longer and it might be a bit harder for you but you will get there (Susan)*
- *(Feeling empowered) taking control is probably that's what it is. Feeling that you were going to take some control rather than have things happen to you.*
- *(Recognising that) I am the expert... but it's having that confidence to know that, that is really valuable (Robert)*
- *Attend meetings with a very good friend or an independent professional, so that to make sure we understand what has been said (Lori)*
- *To be realistic about meetings. There are things I can influence but there are things I can't control, understand the fine line on how I can influence on the things I can't control. I was coming with suggestions instead of saying "I want that" (Susan)*

Topics for Discussion

1. Is resilience something that we are born with or can it be learnt and developed?
2. Since resilience is used as a term in so many different areas of life, how can we explain to parents what it means?
3. How can we enhance a sense of agency in parents and individuals with SEND?
4. If resilience can be learnt, what key concepts do professionals need to consider to support its development for parents?

References

Alaszewski, A. (1998) Risk in modern society. In A. Alaszewski, L. Harrison, & J. Manthorpe (eds.) *Risk, Health and Welfare*. Buckingham: Open University Press.

Allen, T. D., Merlo, K., Lawrence, R. C., Slutsky, J., & Gray, C. E. (2021) Boundary management and work-nonwork balance while working from home. *Applied Psychology*, 70(1), 60–84.

Angelhoff, C., Askenteg, H., Wikner, U., & Edéll-Gustafsson, U. (2018) "To cope with everyday life, I need to sleep"–A phenomenographic study exploring sleep loss in parents of children with Atopic Dermatitis. *Journal of Pediatric Nursing*, 43, e59–e65.

Ben Simon, E., Vallat, R., Rossi, A., & Walker, M. P. (2022) Sleep loss leads to the withdrawal of human helping across individuals, groups, and large-scale societies. *PLoS Biology*, 20(8), e3001733.

Bottrell, D. (2013) Responsibilised resilience? Reworking neoliberal social policy texts. *M/C Journal*, 16, 5–11.

Bull, A., & Allen, K. (2018) Introduction: Sociological interrogations of the turn to character. *Sociological Research Online*, 23(2), 392–398.

Burman, E. (2018) (Re) sourcing the character and resilience manifesto: Suppressions and slippages of (re) presentation and selective affectivities. *Sociological Research Online*, 23(2), 416–437.

Clouston, T. J. (2015). *Challenging Stress, Burnout and Rust-out: Finding Balance in Busy Lives*. London: Jessica Kingsley Publishers.

Coifman, K. G., Bonanno, G. A., & Rafaeli, E. (2007) Affect dynamics, bereavement and resilience to loss. *Journal of Happiness Studies*, 8(3), 371–392.

Cortesi, F., Giannotti, F., Ivanenko, A., & Johnson, K. (2010) Sleep in children with autistic spectrum disorder. *Sleep Medicine*, 11(7), 659–664.

Courtney, E., Kiernan, G., Guerin, S., Ryan, K., & McQuillan, R. (2018). Mothers' perspectives of the experience and impact of caring for their child with a life-limiting neurodevelopmental disability. *Child: Care, Health and Development*, 44(5), 704–710.

Davenport, S., & Zolnikov, T. R. (2021) Understanding mental health outcomes related to compassion fatigue in parents of children diagnosed with intellectual disability. *Journal of Intellectual Disabilities*, https://doi.org/10.1177/17446295211013600.

Dunning, M., Seymour, M., Cooklin, A., & Giallo, R. (2013) Wide awake parenting: Study protocol for a randomised controlled trial of a parenting program for the management of post-partum fatigue. *BMC Public Health*, 13(1), 26.

Estêvão, P., Calado, A., & Capucha, L. (2017) Resilience: Moving from a "heroic" notion to a sociological concept. *Sociologia, Problemas e Práticas*, 85, 9–25.

Evans, B., & Reid, J. (2015) Exhausted by resilience: Response to the commentaries. *Resilience*, 3(2), 154–159.

Evans, G., & Tilley, J. (2016) *The New Class War: The Political and Social Marginalisation of the British Working Class*. Oxford: Oxford University Press.

Everingham, C. (2002) Engendering time: Gender equity and discourses of workplace flexibility. *Time & Society*, 11(2–3), 335–351.

Fenton, J. (2020) 'Four'sa crowd'? Making sense of neoliberalism, ethical stress, moral courage and resilience. *Ethics and Social Welfare*, 14(1), 6–20.

Findler, L., Jacoby, A. K., & Gabis, L. (2016) Subjective happiness among mothers of children with disabilities: The role of stress, attachment, guilt and social support. *Research in Developmental Disabilities*, 55, 44–54.

Fletcher, D., & Sarkar, M. (2013) Psychological resilience: A review and critique of definitions, concepts, and theory. *European Psychologist*, 18(1), 12.

Frankl, V. (1959) *Man's Search for Meaning*. New York: Washington Square Press.

Garmezy, N. (1993) Children in poverty: Resilience despite risk. *Psychiatry*, 56(1), 127–136.

Giallo, R., Rose, N., & Vittorino, R. (2011) Fatigue, wellbeing and parenting in mothers of infants and toddlers with sleep problems. *Journal of Reproductive and Infant Psychology*, 29(3), 236–249.

Gill, R., & Orgad, S. (2018) The Amazing Bounce-Backable Woman: Resilience and the Psychological Turn in Neoliberalism. *Sociological Research Online*, 23(2), 477–495.

Gröpel, P., & Kuhl, J. (2009) Work–life balance and subjective well-being: The mediating role of need fulfilment. *British Journal of Psychology*, 100(2), 365–375.

Grotberg, E. (1997) The international resilience project. *A Charge Against Society: The Child's Right to Protection*, pp. 19–32.

Hart, A., Heaver, B., Brunnberg, E., Sandberg, A., Macpherson, H., Coombe, S., & Kourkoutas, E. (2014) Resilience-building with disabled children and young people: A review and critique of the academic evidence base. *International Journal of Child, Youth and Family Studies*, 5(3), 394–422.

Hasan, Z. U., Khan, M. I., Butt, T. H., Abid, G., & Rehman, S. (2020) The balance between work and life for subjective well-being: A moderated mediation model. *Journal of Open Innovation: Technology, Market, and Complexity*, 6(4), 127.

Hammell, K. W. (2004) Dimensions of meaning in the occupations of daily life. *Canadian Journal of Occupational Therapy*, 71(5), 296–305.

Heiman, T. (2002) Parents of children with disabilities: Resilience, coping, and future expectations. *Journal of developmental and physical disabilities*, 14(2), 159–171.

Hickman, P. (2018) A flawed construct? Understanding and unpicking the concept of resilience in the context of economic hardship. *Social Policy and Society*, 17(3), 409–424.

Hochschild, A. R. (1997) When work becomes home and home becomes work. *California Management Review*, 39(4), 79.

Hochschild, A. R. (2007) Through the crack of the time bind: From market management to family management. *Anthropology of Work Review*, 28(1), 1–8.

Hochschild, A. R. (2012) *The Managed Heart: Commercialization of Human Feeling*. Berkeley: University of California Press.

Hochschild, A. R. (2013) *So How's the Family?: And Other Essays*. Berkeley: University of California Press.

Hornby, G. (1992) A review of fathers' accounts of their experiences of parenting children with disabilities. *Disability, Handicap & Society*, 7(4), 363–374.

Hughes, J. M., Ulmer, C. S., Hastings, S. N., Gierisch, J. M., Workgroup, M.-A. V. M., & Howard, M. O. (2018) Sleep, resilience, and psychological distress in United States military Veterans. *Military Psychology*, 30(5), 404–414.

Keville, S., Meek, C., & Ludlow, A. K. (2021) Mothers' perspectives of co-occurring fatigue in children with autism spectrum disorders. *Fatigue: Biomedicine, Health & Behavior*, 9(4), 209–226.

Kienhuis, M., Rogers, S., Giallo, R., Matthews, J., & Treyvaud, K. (2010). A proposed model for the impact of parental fatigue on parenting adaptability and child development. *Journal of Reproductive and Infant Psychology*, 28(4), 392–402.

Kinman, G., & Grant, L. (2010) Exploring stress resilience in trainee social workers: The role of emotional and social competencies. *The British Journal of Social Work*, 41(2), 261–275.

Knight, K. (2013). The changing face of the 'good mother': Trends in research into families with a child with intellectual disability, and some concerns. *Disability & Society*, 28(5), 660–673.

Lewis, S., & Beauregard, T. (2018) The meanings of work-life balance: A cultural perspective. In K. Shockley, W. Shen, & R. Johnson (eds.) *The Cambridge Handbook of the Global Work-Family Interface*. Cambridge Handbooks in Psychology. Cambridge: Cambridge University Press, pp. 720–732.

Littler, J. (2013) Meritocracy as plutocracy: The marketising of 'equality' within neoliberalism. *New Formations: A Journal of Culture/Theory/Politics*, 80–81, pp. 52–72. https://doi.org/10.3898/NewF.80/81.03.2013

Lown, M., Lewith, G., Simon, C., & Peters, D. (2015) Resilience: What is it, why do we need it, and can it help us? *British Journal of General Practice*, 65(639), e708–e710.

Maher, C., Crettenden, A., Evans, K., Thiessen, M., Toohey, M., Watson, A., & Dollman, J. (2015) Fatigue is a major issue for children and adolescents with physical disabilities. *Developmental Medicine & Child Neurology*, 57(8), 742–747.

Manoudi, A., Weber, T., Scott, D., & Hawley Woodall, J. (2018) An analysis of Personal and Household Services to support work life balance for working parents and carers. *Synthesis Report. ECE Thematic Review*.

Mantua, J., Brager, A. J., Alger, S. E., Adewale, F., Skeiky, L., Balkin, T. J.,... & Simonelli, G. (2021) Self-reported sleep need, subjective resilience, and cognitive performance following sleep loss and recovery sleep. *Psychological Reports*, 124(1), 210–226.

Maslach, C., & Jackson, S. (1981) The measurement of experienced burnout. *Journal of Occupational Behavior*, 2, 99–113.

Maslach, C. A., Jackson, S. E., & Leiter, M. (1997) *The Truth About Burnout*. San Francisco, CA: Jossey-Bass.

Masten, A. S. (2015) *Ordinary Magic: Resilience in Development*. London: Guilford Publications.

Matheson, R., Judd-Lam, S., Gleeson, P., & Viswanathan, P. (2020) Working remotely can work for carers but multi-dimensional flexibility will even better meet their needs Available at: https://carersandemployers.org.au/uploads/main/News/CarersEmployers_Briefing_2-Flexible-Working-Nov-2020.pdf

Mazurek, M. O., & Petroski, G. F. (2015) Sleep problems in children with autism spectrum disorder: Examining the contributions of sensor over-responsivity and anxiety. *Sleep Medicine*, 16, 270–279.

McRobbie, A. (2020) *Feminism and the Politics of Resilience: Essays on Gender, Media and the End of Welfare*. Chichester: John Wiley & Sons.

Micsinszki, S. K., Ballantyne, M., Cleverley, K., Green, P., & Stremler, R. (2018) Sleep outcomes for parents of children with neurodevelopmental disabilities: A systematic review. *Journal of Family Nursing*, 24(2), 217–249.

Mireku, M. (2021) Waking activities and sleep: Analysis of UK adolescents' daily time-use diaries. *Journal of Adolescent Health*, 68(2), 385–393

Nixon, C. D., & Singer, G. H. (2002) Group cognitive-behavioral treatment for excessive parental self-blame and guilt. *The Best of AAMR: Families and Mental Retardation: A Collection of Notable AAMR Journal Articles Across the 20th Century*, 331.

Osborne, L. A., & Reed, P. (2008) Parents' perceptions of communication with professionals during the diagnosis of autism. *Autism: The International Journal of Research and Practice*, 12, 309–324. https://doi.org/10.1177/1362361307089517

Patterson, J. L., Goens, G. A., & Reed, D. E. (2009) *Resilient Leadership for Turbulent Times: A Guide to Thriving in the Face of Adversity*. Washington DC: R&L Education.

Pietrzak, R. H., & Southwick, S. M. (2011) Psychological resilience in OEF-OIF Veterans: Application of a novel classification approach and examination of demographic and psychosocial correlates. *Journal of Affect Disorders*, 133(3), 560–568.

Pignatiello, G. A., Martin, R. J., & Hickman Jr., R. L. (2020) Decision fatigue: A conceptual analysis. *Journal of Health Psychology*, 25(1), 123–135.

Rufat, S. (2015) Critique of pure resilience. In *Resilience Imperative*. Oxford: Elsevier Ltd, 201–228.

Ryan, C., & Quinlan, E. (2018) Whoever shouts the loudest: Listening to parents of children with disabilities. *Journal of Applied Research in Intellectual Disabilities*, 31, 203–214.

Salceanu, C., & Luminita, S. M. (2020) Anxiety and depression in parents of disabled children. *Technium Social Sciences Journal*, 3, 141.

Seccombe, K. (2002) "Beating the odds" versus "changing the odds": Poverty, resilience, and family policy. *Journal of Marriage and Family*, 64(2), 384–394.

Seymour, M., Wood, C., Giallo, R., & Jellett, R. (2013) Fatigue, stress and coping in mothers of children with an autism spectrum disorder. *Journal of Autism and Developmental Disorders*, 43(7), 1547–1554.

Smethurst, C. (2017) Class inequality and social work: We're all in this together. In K. Bhatti-Sinclair & C. Smethurst (eds.) *Diversity Difference and Professional Dilemmas: Developing Skills in Challenging Times*. London: Open University McGraw Hill.

Sollisch, J. (2016) The cure for decision fatigue. *Wall Street Journal*, 10.

Southwick, S. M., Bonanno, G. A., Masten, A. S., Panter-Brick, C., & Yehuda, R. (2014) Resilience definitions, theory, and challenges: Interdisciplinary perspectives. *European Journal of Psychotraumatology*, 5(1), 25338.

Taşan-Kok, T., Stead, D., & Lu, P. (2013) Conceptual overview of resilience: History and context. *Resilience Thinking in Urban Planning*, 106, 39–51.

Theorell, T. (2020) The demand control support work stress model. *Handbook of Socioeconomic Determinants of Occupational Health: From Macro-level to Micro-level Evidence*, 339–353. Cham: Springer, Available at: https://doi.org/10.1007/978-3-030-31438-5_13

Tierney, J. (2011) Do you suffer from decision fatigue. *The New York Times*, 17.

Van der Kolk, B. (2014) *The Body Keeps the Score: Mind, Brain and Body in the Transformation of Trauma*. Harmondsworth: Penguin.

Van Dongen, H., Maislin, G., Mullington, J. M., & Dinges, D. F. (2003). The cumulative cost of additional wakefulness: dose-response effects on neurobehavioral functions and sleep physiology from chronic sleep restriction and total sleep deprivation. *Sleep*, 26(2), 117–126.

Vasquez, R. (2022) You just need more resilience: Racial gaslighting as "Othering". *Journal of Critical Thought and Praxis*, 11(3), Article 5.

Wade, C. M., Mildon, R. L., & Matthews, J. M. (2007) Service delivery to parents with an intellectual disability: Family-centred or professionally centred? *Journal of Applied Research in Intellectual Disabilities*, 20(2), 87–98.

Walker, M. (2017) *Why We Sleep: Unlocking the Power of Sleep and Dreams*. London: Simon and Schuster.

Walker, J., & Cooper, M. (2011) Genealogies of resilience: From systems ecology to the political economy of crisis adaptation. *Security Dialogue*, 42(2), 143–160.

Walsh, F. (2003) Family resilience: A framework for clinical practice. *Family Process*, 42(1), 1–18.

Watson, N. F. et al. (2015) Recommended amount of sleep for a healthy adult: A joint consensus statement of the American Academy of Sleep Medicine and Sleep Research Society. *Sleep*, 38(6), 843–844.

Wilcock, A. A. (1999) Reflections on doing, being and becoming. *Australian Occupational Therapy Journal*, 46(1), 1–11.

Yeandle, S. (2020) *Peer Review on 'Work–life Balance: Promoting Gender Equality in Informal Long-Term Care Provision'*. Thematic Discussion Paper, European Commission, DG Employment, Social Affairs and Inclusion.

9 True Partnerships, Can They Work?

Introduction

True Partnerships: Are They Possible?

Like so much of the terminology linked to SEND, partnership working is in danger of becoming an over-used, under-worked and tokenistic concept. Formal partnerships can be made between individuals, groups or organisations (Balloch & Taylor, 2001). A true partnership, however, involves more than making sure that a parent or individual with SEND has been informed of what is happening, or are sitting in the room when decisions are made. True partnerships must go beyond a meeting room (or virtual space) and must represent an emotional as well as an "official" connection. Formally, the current understanding of partnership working includes the concept of co-production and co-creation and is linked to the emergence of the social model of disability (Oliver, 1986). Effective co-production involves mutual respect and putting the needs of those with SEND and their families at the heart of any decisions made about them. This is supported through legislation in the Children and Families Act (2014) and rooted in the UPIAS motto from the 1980s, "nothing about us without us". For co-production to be effective, the views of all participants must be given equal value, and communication must be clear, honest and jargon-free. But the basis of a true partnership depends on more than being given a platform and a voice. Time and again, when interviewing for this book, parents have made it clear that what is most important to them is the creation of trusting relationships based on mutual respect, a holistic understanding of their lived experience and interest in their child. Where partnerships have worked well, professionals have shown empathy and, most importantly, have taken time, despite heavy caseloads, time constraints and financial limitations, to get to know the families and to listen to and understand the children, young people and adults they are working with.

> I guess what I was trying to say… is that professionals who are Jonathan-focused tend to be the ones who get the best working relationship with me and whose work ultimately makes a difference. I joke… that my world is divided quite neatly into those people who value Jonathan, and those who don't – I guess it's a protective mechanism, but really, I learnt quite early that people who 'speak' to Jonathan (whether or not they get anything back) are those who are worth my time.
>
> (Susan)

This final chapter pulls together the emerging themes from our interviews, explores the hopes of parents and professionals and imagines how these can be used to develop consistently positive future partnerships.

What Parents Hope For

To Be Listened To

A constantly re-emerging theme from the interviews is the wish to be listened to.

> Listen to parents that's one of the things it's not just that paperwork, it is the individuals behind the paperwork as well
>
> (Robert)

DOI: 10.4324/9781003089506-10

So yeah listen, just listen I think that's the main thing. And don't just hear it, listen to it.

(Hannah)

Listen. Don't judge… every single person and every single situation is unique

(Jono)

Listen to the parents because at the end of the day, even if you spend 4 hours assessing a child, a parent spends a lifetime with them

(Nigel)

Feeling listened to is fundamental to the development of true partnerships. Believing that your voice is heard and that your views are valued links to Schlossberg's (1989) concept of "mattering", of believing that what we say is of importance and interest to others (Marshall, 2001; Rosenberg & McCullough, 1981). The skill of listening with empathy, understanding and whole-heartedness (Brown, 2012) is key to the development of the trusting relationship that must form the basis of any partnership, whether personal or professional.

Professionals Who Care Enough

Time and again, parents talk about successful parent/professional partnerships in terms of the extent to which therapists, social workers or SENCOs seem to care about them and their family and listen to their children.

Where positive relationships have been built, they are with professionals who care enough, who take time to get to know the family and the individual and who seem to have an innate understanding of what is needed. Partnerships work where personal skills are prioritised over professional knowledge, where the individual is the focus rather than the process and where people bring their heart as well as their knowledge and expertise into the relationship. This does not imply that professional boundaries should be crossed but rather that partnerships need to be based on compassion, empathy and understanding.

I had a really nice health visitor. ……She was really really nice and I think she, she gave me special attention. She would always come and visit me at home rather than me going to her clinic, … I didn't really want to go out initially.

(Dana)

the professionals where you felt you've got the most support, were the professionals who actually cared, with that more holistic… more rounded, more thoughtful understanding.

(Jono)

some people are just able to make those connections or understand that what they're bringing is not just their knowledge…, it's about a lot more than that. It's about being able to connect with people

(Tessa)

Open and Honest Communication

The Lamb Inquiry (2009) highlights the importance of good, honest and open communication, yet interviewees often feel that professionals, perhaps because of limited resources or prescriptive organisational agendas, are not always able to be as open or as honest as parents wish them to be. Parents understand that professionals cannot know the answers to everything but accessibility, knowing that they are available to offer advice, that phone calls will be returned and that emails will be answered within a realistic timeframe, plays a large part in the development of trusting relationships.

and I think this is something that's really important…. the sharing of information and resources

(Tessa)

This echoes the findings of Mittler and Mittler (1982) that partnerships must be based on a full sharing of knowledge and experience.

For parents, struggling to come to terms with continual transitions between schools, colleges, services and funding sources, knowing that they can trust professionals to support them, to explain clearly what needs to be done in language free from jargon and acronyms, means a great deal. While legislation supports the rights of parents and individuals with disabilities to shape their own futures, the paperwork, procedures and meetings involved are often daunting and confusing. Professionals who empower individuals and families to navigate the system and who help to give them the confidence they need to be pro-active participants in their own futures, lead the way in the development of true partnerships.

> the most important thing is help with navigating ... the system. It would just be really nice if somebody helped you right from the start and told you everything that was available and helped you with those things, like benefits, the paperwork.
>
> (Dana)

Honest, open and equal conversations enable families to gain a clear understanding of what professionals are able to do (and to acknowledge what they are not able to do). By gaining the trust of parents, professionals gain a more honest perspective of their lived experience and of their role as experts on their children (Cheminais, 2011; Nutbrown et al., 2013; Dyson et al, 2004).

Focus on Capabilities Not Disabilities

In order to ensure children and young people receive the correct support and funding, parents and professionals can find themselves focusing on deficits, on what their children are unable to do. Successes are often underplayed or overlooked because they could lead to a reduction of support or the removal of services. For parents, this focus on deficits rather than strengths can lead to a loss of hope and a triggering of chronic sorrow.

> The physio said, 'oh look at what she can do. Look she can do this and this,' and it was the first time that anybody had said something positive about her abilities and we were just blown away and in tears
>
> (Tessa)

Co-produced, person-centred plans should mean that potential outcomes are built on capabilities rather than disabilities, ensuring that individuals move forwards at their own speed and in their own time.

This recognition of the individual rather than the impairment is key to effective partnerships. Talking to the child or adult, ensuring they are not perceived as "lesser" (Lori), acknowledging that their views are valued, that they have just as much right to hope and dream as anyone else, is essential to partnership building for both those with impairments and their parents.

> Don't focus on the disabilities, we already do that,... we know what our children might not do in life and that is the fear that drives us everyday. But we also know what our children can do and encourage us to also dream, you know, just give us it that hope and aspiration, that you know the best that we wish for our children can be a reality that they can have in their lifetime.
>
> (Robert)

> I wish people could really see [our daughter] for who she is and what she's able to do.
>
> (Tessa)

Equality of Opportunity

Many of the parents interviewed believe that the current system does not represent equality for all. They feel that families from higher socio-economic backgrounds with money and social confidence are more likely to gain the outcomes they want for their children with SEND. For those from ethnic minorities and/or lower socio-economic backgrounds with less confidence to speak as equals with professionals and often less awareness of how to access services or appeal decisions, the co-productive process can appear too daunting, the paperwork too complicated and the system too confusing.

> I would love to be able to think of a way to make the system more equal. ... everything that we have gained ... has been gained sort of unfairly ... because we come from privilege.

(Ava)

Creating a more equitable SEND system needs to be recognised as a key priority for professionals. True partnerships in SEND depend on giving a voice to the voiceless, empowering the disempowered and ensuring that inclusion and acceptance form the basis of any support systems that are put in place. Without greater equity, this cannot happen.

What Professionals Hope for?

To Have More Time to Listen

Making time for regular meetings with parents and listening to their views can be a real challenge when the professional has many responsibilities to fulfil in their working week; it is possible, however, that long-term this can save time.

> "although listening to parents is time-consuming ... it saves me a lot of time and a great deal of potential unpleasantness later!."

(SENCO, 2019)

To Have Time to Build Trusting Relationship

Fox et al. (2017) identify that good communication is a key to effective partnerships between parents and educational staff. "Good communication" has been placed at the heart of an approach to parent partnership working by Maggie MacDonnell, a Global Teacher prize winner. MacDonnell (2018) believes asking for permission, and for an invitation, to become involved in their child's life is a key starting point in connecting with parents, guardians and family members. There is no assumption of a position of authority. MacDonnell goes on to explain that she asks for their permission to visit the family at home. She asks families to share insights about their children, their likes, hobbies, interests and stressors. She shares expectations and asks for their advice and input. She also starts off each year with several deliberate positive interactions with the parent, trying to find informal ways to come together and build connections. MacDonnell also believes that keeping herself visible and participating in community events is a useful way to connect informally with parents. This last point made by MacDonnell concurs with the first point made by educational professionals, who state that "being visible" is a key strategy towards effective partnership.

To Ensure that the Language Used Is Understandable to All

From information gathered in interviews, "variations in language and terminology" has also been identified as a theme. Parents and professionals alike can find the jargon and paperwork too confusing. Reports from professionals can be saturated with technical language and acronyms. Often such technical language and terminology are specific to each group of professionals within either education, health or the social care sectors. It could be suggested that deciphering and understanding what is meant by such specific terminology can often contribute to a resistance of collaborative working. This may then result in a time delay of the child's or young person's needs being met. Fox et al. (2017) take this point further in considering not just technical terminology in isolation, but the challenge of considering specific diagnosis and labels of conditions. They suggest that community attitudes towards mental illness, challenging behaviours and disability, combined with the lack of vocabulary to describe and explain certain conditions, i.e., autism, can make acceptance by parents extremely challenging. It can therefore be difficult for parents to recognise that their child's disability may be characteristic to certain conditions, for example, autism. These attitudes can also prevent parents from sharing their concerns about their child, meaning that assessment and diagnosis can sometimes be delayed (Fox et al., 2017).

Professionals' Views on Perceived Challenges to Partnership Working

When asked what they perceived to be the main challenges to effective partnership working, with parents, professionals highlight a lack of understanding by parents of the level of support that schools and settings are able to offer. They find that managing expectations, often coupled with misunderstanding of SEND entitlement, means that parents often feel let down by professionals. This is especially true when parents feel that their child should have an EHCP but professionals do not. For those working with the families, finding a time to meet that is convenient for all can be difficult and is especially hard when families are reluctant to engage. This is exacerbated by the fact that contact with parents is hard to maintain since their children often travel to and from settings by bus or taxi. As is reflected in the views of the parents, jargon, paperwork and a lack of shared language are considered to be a challenge for both inter-agency working, co-production and building meaningful partnerships. Perhaps one of the greatest challenges to the creation of true partnerships between professionals and parents is the sometimes seemingly adversarial approach of the parents. Parents often seem angry or defensive, the fight response dominating their interactions. As discussed throughout this book, understanding the lived experience of parents, that they often feel they have been doing battle since receiving the diagnosis of impairment, can help professionals to act with empathy and compassion, rather than responding defensively. Such actions prevent escalation and polarisation.

Whilst recognition of the role of parents has grown inexorably over the last 50 years, the sense that they are in a constant state of war with the system and the professionals who represent it remains strong. Effective co-production depends on a clear understanding of the lived experience of parents and acknowledgement, from both sides, of the true meaning of partnership. Building true partnership takes time and emotional effort. Trusting relationships must be developed, mutual expertise acknowledged and a shared vision created. But the time invested in creating partnerships based on equality and mutual respect is an investment in a better future and raising aspirations for each child with SEND.

> "It is possible to find ways to open up our working. We can create situations which support people to work with a variety of others. And by attempting to do these kinds of things, we will create moments, new opportunities which will lead us … somewhere… together."
>
> (Rix, 2021, p.7)

Professional Awareness of What Works

A small study carried out with professionals by the authors highlights a shared understanding of what is necessary to ensure open and trusting relationships can be achieved. Of key interest is the overlap between what they understand to be important and what our interviews and research have shown that parents hope for from professionals. Below is the list:

- Being visible
- Keeping regularly in touch
- Making time to listen
- Being honest
- Responding quickly
- Including parents in meetings
- Showing interest in their child
- Recognising the parent as the expert
- Ensuring approaches are consistent
- Using structured conversations
- Allowing time and space to vent for both professionals and parents
- Asking a colleague join difficult conversation
- Keeping calm
- Having an open-door policy

One key challenge of collaborative working with parents is to ensure SEND systems can accommodate those who want to be active participants in their child's education, but not marginalise those who do not have the time or resources to do the same.

Conclusion

Writing this book has taken us on a journey that has been both humbling and moving. We have spoken to parents who find every day a battle and those who feel, to some extent at least, that they have received the support they needed. Each of the families interviewed have told us stories of times when partnerships with professionals have failed but when they have worked, their gratitude and relief is almost tangible. As our society transitions (too) slowly from the medical to the social model; as legislation prioritises co-production and person-centred decision-making, as new generations grow up better understanding what those with disabilities bring to rather than what they take from, the world, as many professionals try their hardest to ensure that the voice of those with SEND is heard, there is hope that true and strong partnerships can be formed. The journey towards inclusion and acceptance will never end but the possibility of true partnerships based on empathy, compassion and understanding will help to build resilience and make the challenges easier to overcome.

> I remember, one sports day when James ran in the opposite direction to everyone else as in right the other field away, I remember just thinking this is the journey that you go on with a child with special needs, you always feel like you're running in a different direction.
>
> (Susan)

Whatever the starting point, it is our job, as professionals, to run beside individuals with SEND, in whichever direction they choose. True partnerships must originate in a shared vision based on better outcomes for all – that is the beginning and end of the race we are running together.

Creating True Partnerships: Final Takeaways

- Allow time and space for true partnerships to develop
- Recognise individual capabilities – emphasise the "can do" rather than a deficit view
- Ensure that collaborative decisions are based on the social not the medical model
- Ensure that the views of everyone are included
- Be receptive to each other's ideas
- Ensure decisions are not based on a tokenistic rhetoric but on overcoming societal barriers
- Recognise that parents are experts on their own children but that they value honest and constructive input and advice
- Recognise triggers of chronic sorrow
- Ensure that individuals and families become pro-active co-producers of their own aspirational and empowering outcomes
- Ensure that communication is clear, accessible and jargon-free

---

Topics for Discussion

1. What is meant by "true partnerships"?
2. What are the challenges that might prevent true partnerships from happening?
3. What can professionals do to ensure partnership working is effective?
4. What can parents do to ensure that partnership working is effective?

References

Balloch, S., & Taylor, M. eds. (2001) *Partnership Working: Policy and Practice*. Bristol: Policy Press.

Brown, B. (2012) The Power of Vulnerability: Teachings on Authenticity, Connection and Courage. Available at: http://www.casesenzaconfini.com/sites/default/files/webform/pdf/pdf-the-power-of-vulnerability-teachings-on-authenticity-connection-brene-brown-pdf-download-free-book-78b1cf2.pdf (Accessed 2 June 2022)

Cheminais, R. (2011) *Family Partnership Working: A Guide for Education Practitioners*. London: Sage.

Children and Families Act (2014) Available at: https://www.legislation.gov.uk/ukpga/2014/6/contents/enacted

Dyson, A., Farrell, P., Polat, F., Hutcheson, G., & Gallannaugh, F. (2004) *Inclusion and Pupil Achievement*. London: DfES.

Fox, F. et al. (2017) "It was like walking without knowing where I was going": A qualitative study of autism in a UK Somali migrant community. *Journal of Autism Developmental Disorders*, 47, 305–315.

Lamb, B. (2009) *Lamb Inquiry, Special Educational Needs and Parental Confidence*. London: DCFS.

MacDonnell, M. (2018) In D. Bartram OBE (ed.) *Great Expectations; Leading an Effective SEND Strategy in School*. Woodbridge: John Catt, pp. 56–59.

Marshall, S. (2001) Do I matter? Construct validation of adolescents' perceived mattering to parents and friends. *Journal of adolescence*, 24(4), 473–490.

Mittler, P., & Mittler, H. (1982) *Partnership with Parents*. Stratford-upon-Avon: National Council for Special Education.

Nutbrown, C., Clough, P., & Atherton, F. (2013) *Inclusion in the Early Years*. London: Sage.

Oliver, M. (1986) Social policy and disability: Some theoretical issues. *Disability, Handicap & Society*, 1(1), 5–17.

Rix, J. (2021) Inclusive relationships: Creating the space for each other. In M. Beaton, G. Codina, & J. Wharton (eds.) *Leading on Inclusion: The Role of the SENCO*. Abingdon: Routledge, pp. 7–14.

Rosenberg, M., & McCullough, B. C. (1981) Mattering: Inferred significance and mental health among adolescents. *Research in Community & Mental Health*, 2, 163–182.

Schlossberg, N. K. (1989) Marginality and mattering: Key issues in building community. *New Directions for Student Services*, 1989(48), 5–15.

Imagining True Partnerships

Imagine a partnership where everyone has a voice that is equally valued

Imagine a partnership based on aspirations and hope, whatever your need or ability

Imagine a partnership based on mutual respect

Imagine a partnership based on time to care enough

Imagine a partnership based on empathy and compassion

> I remember, one sports day when Thomas ran in the opposite direction to everyone else as in right the other field away, I remember just thinking this is the journey that you go on with a child with special needs, you always feel like you're running in a different direction.
>
> (Susan)

Wherever the journey begins, it is our job, as professionals, to run with individuals with SEND, whatever path they choose to follow. True partnerships must originate in a shared vision based on better outcomes for all – that is the beginning and end of the race we are running together.

Index

Note: **Bold** page numbers refer to tables and *italic* page numbers refer to figures

For Product Safety Concerns and Information please contact our EU representative GPSR@taylorandfrancis.com Taylor & Francis Verlag GmbH, Kaufingerstraße 24, 80331 München, Germany